by

ADAM HOPKINS

Adam Hopkins is a travel writer and regular contributor to the
Sunday Times and The Guardian. He is the author of books on
Holland and Crete.

AA

Produced by the Publishing Division of
The Automobile Association

Written by Adam Hopkins
Peace and Quiet section by Paul
Sterry
Consultant: Frank Dawes

Edited, designed and produced by
the Publishing Division of The
Automobile Association. Maps ©
The Automobile Association 1990

Distributed in the United Kingdom
by the Publishing Division of The
Automobile Association, Fanum
House, Basingstoke, Hampshire,
RG21 2EA

The contents of this publication are
believed correct at the time of
printing. Nevertheless, the
publishers cannot accept
responsibility for errors or
omissions, nor for changes in details
given.

A CIP catalogue record for this book
is available from the British Library.

ISBN 0 86145 872 9

Published by The Automobile
Association

Typesetting: Tradespools Ltd, Frome,
Somerset
Colour separation: L C Repro,
Aldermaston
Printing: Printers S.R.L., Trento, Italy

Front cover: Ayia Galini

Greek place names can be transcribed in various ways and some appear in the text in two different forms. Where this occurs, the version in brackets is the form used on the maps.

This book employs a simple rating system to help choose which places to visit:

◆◆◆   do not miss

◆◆   see if you can

◆   worth seeing if you have time

INTRODUCTION

INTRODUCTION

Crete is an island which is truly special, one of the strong places of the earth. Few can visit it, even for simple sun and sea, and return to their homes indifferent. Its people are dignified and generous; its mountains are rugged and visible everywhere; its fertile spots, though fewer, have a luxurious abundance. The island is lapped by many miles of beach, particularly along the north, with bay and cliff as dramatic interludes. It has a past which goes back well before the conscious memory of man.

The Minoans flourished here centuries before classical Greece. Theirs was the earliest of the great civilisations on European soil; and one of the pleasures of a visit to Crete is to make the acquaintance of their art and artefacts and the remains of their fine buildings. This was the civilisation which made a cult of the wild bull and gave rise to the extraordinary legends of Minos, the Minotaur and the Labyrinth of Knossos. Crete had great importance in classical mythology. The ancient Greeks left ruins behind them here as well as the Minoans. So did the Romans and the Byzantines, the Venetians who ruled the island for four centuries, and the Turks who held power for a further two. The modern Cretans, successors to this great avalanche of history, only became part of the modern Greek nation in 1913.

Ancient Crete was fertile and wealthy. Modern Crete is mostly harsh and rocky; World War II brought outright tragedy to a poor land. The defeat of the Allies here was followed by bitter repression under the Germans as the Cretans strove to wage a war of resistance. Better times have come just lately, however, with the arrival of international tourism. Through all this the Cretans have maintained a tradition of hospitality and welcome which appears to go back in an unbroken line, for three millennia at least, to the Bronze Age of the eastern Mediterranean. Crete has still in many ways and places the largeness of spirit evident in the epic tales of Homer— not that anyone should form too favourable an advance picture. Some of the best aspects of Crete are slow to reveal themselves. The splendour of the mountains may be felt at once, but the island is hot in summer and certainly seems dusty if you arrive in Iraklion, the capital. And Iraklion is astonishingly ugly. Many of Crete's hotels—the great majority of them along the beaches and bays of the north coast—are fine and comfortable, but some of the more recent building in tourist areas is flimsy, brash and unco-ordinated. Along the south coast, and now creeping into parts of the north, there are multitudinous greenhouses covered in plastic sheeting which decays in winter. Moreover, the island is so rugged and parts of it still so inaccessible, despite a rapid improvement in the roads, that even with the best will in the world it would take many weeks to see every corner. Yet it is often in the most out-of-the-way places that Crete remains at its finest.

These are the complicating factors. In practice, most people take their first steps towards the deeper Crete within a very few days or hours, either through the discovery of landscape and villages or through their meetings with local people. Often, departing visitors, brown as berries from the beach, rate the friendliness of the Cretans beyond all the other pleasures of the island. For better or worse, those who come to know Crete well are never quite free of it again.

BACKGROUND

The Landscape

It is hard to make sense of Crete without some understanding of its unusual and dramatic physical construction. The island is long and thin—some 150 miles (250km) from east to west and 10 miles (15km) or so to 40 miles (60km) wide.

Often known as the *Megali Nisi* or Great Island, it is easily the largest of the Greek islands. There are three main towns strung out along the northern coast—Khania in the extreme west, Rethimnon in centre west and Iraklion, considerably the largest, almost at dead centre. The true tourist capital, though, is Ayios Nikolaos, halfway along towards the eastern end and looking out over a wide gulf. Agreeable little Sitia, to the east, was formerly one of the main towns, but it is hard to rate in the top league today. The major towns of the north coast and the coastal plain which links them, effectively from west of Khania to Ayios Nikolaos in the east, together have the bulk of the population and welcome the majority of tourists. Visually, though, it is the mountains which dominate. Being made of limestone, they are rugged and austere, mountainous far beyond their real size in the impression they create. As with the major towns, the mountain ranges come in a set of four. The finest and by far the wildest are the White Mountains or Lefka Ori in the west, lying more or less south of Khania. This is a terrain of gorges, crags and screes, treacherous to the inexperienced walker, inspiring to those who get to know its ways. Like most of the ranges, it hides high flat plains close to its heart.

Next along towards the centre of the island, lying well back from the coast between Rethimnon and Iraklion, there rises the bulk of Psiloritis (once better known as Ida), more a single mountain than a range, though pierced by extremely attractive high valleys. The highest peak of Psiloritis is by a whisker the highest point on Crete—8,058ft (2,456m) compared to the 8,045ft (2,452m) of Pachnes, top spot in the White Mountains.

The lofty clump of mountain surging up south and west of Ayios Nikolaos is the Dikte massif.

Tourism and tradition: an old way of life meets new demands

Both Psiloritis and Dikte possess caves which are immensely important in classical Greek myth; and Dikte also possesses in the Lasithi Plateau, right in its centre, the most extensive and remarkable of Crete's high plains. The southern part of the massif is particularly beautiful.

The final range, lower but still impressive, is round Sitia in the east. The mountains here hide interesting villages and lesser known prehistoric and historic sites. In many of the villages ancient ways of life persist.

From anywhere in Crete, and especially from the beaches, you are likely to see at least one of these ranges. Mountains, one feels, are what matter most in Crete. The richest part of the island agriculturally, however, lies south of the main mountain groups, in the central area of Crete. This is the Plain of Mesara, with huge and ancient olive trees and now many younger ones as well. The visitor will cross the Mesara to reach some of Crete's finest archaeological sites and, towards the west, a good view of innumerable plastic greenhouses. These produce several crops a year, running well ahead of the seasons. Among the crops are tomatoes, cucumbers, melons, and even kiwi fruit; bananas also grow profusely in Cretan greenhouses. In addition to the Mesara, there are other smaller areas which are also extremely fertile, their sense of ease and abundance contrasting most forcefully with the rigour of the rest of the island. Apart from the greenhouse crops, Crete's traditional staples are grapes and the ubiquitous lowland olive. Carob trees, smaller than olives and yielding dark-coloured, bean-like pods, are also very common, especially in the east. The beans are used mainly for animal fodder.

Crete's most extensive beaches lie along the northern coast where tourist development is concentrated. There are many miles of sand, some sand and shingle, some areas of rock well used by swimmers. Both the extreme east and west coasts have a few outstanding beaches though some of these are less accessible. There are pockets of exceedingly fine beach along the south of the island.

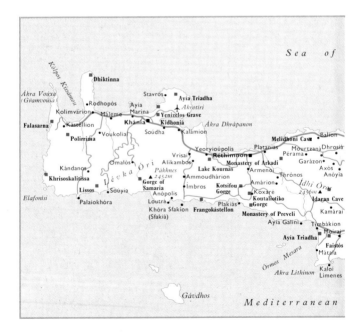

The Minoans

Something extraordinary began to happen in
Crete almost 5,000 years ago, in about 3000BC.
Perhaps it was to do with the seclusion of the
island, the distances of sea that had to be
traversed by new arrivals; perhaps it was in part
the natural wealth of the land—Crete in ancient
times was thickly forested and well-watered;
perhaps it was to do with the nature of the
island's first inhabitants or of the new immigrants
now joining them from the east. Whatever the
reason, from nearly imperceptible beginnings, a
highly individual civilisation took shape.
Neolithic people had first reached Crete some
3,000 years before, in about 6000BC. Their main
settlement was at Knossos, near modern
Iraklion. Otherwise they lived mostly in caves
and refuges. But round about 2600BC, many
settlements moved down to the sea, suggesting
a new confidence and sense of security. This
was indispensable for future developments.
Perhaps the leading characteristic of the whole

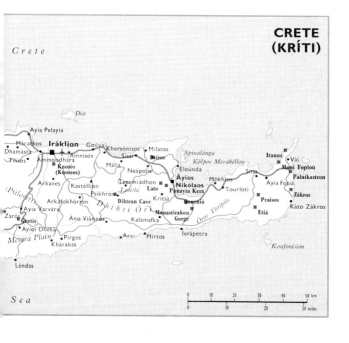

BACKGROUND

Minoan civilisation is that its development appears to have gone hand in hand with peace and prosperity. Its artists, so far as is known, never showed scenes of war; its towns and, later, its palaces, were undefended.

The early Minoans (as we know them now), flourishing particularly in the east and then a little later in the Mesara, were brilliant potters. They carved beautiful stone jars, some with lively animal motifs, and worked in ivory and rock crystal. From an early period they were making quite remarkable, and amazingly beautiful, miniature designs on sealstones.

Pottery is the great stand-by in understanding and discussing prehistoric societies. It is the most durable of materials, and the least likely to be removed from any site, having little value compared to jewellery or weapons and none at all when it is broken. It was used by archaeologists in Crete as elsewhere for the dating of other artefacts and establishing the sequence of developments. This makes it seem natural to open discussion of Minoan periods by talking of pottery styles. But an even better reason is that the pottery from most Minoan periods was exceptionally lovely. There is little from any other time or place to rival it.

Only 600 years from its beginning, Minoan society was constructing a series of vast palaces. Some of the great triumphs of the Minoan potters were achieved in the time of the first palaces, from 1900 to 1700BC; there are many examples in the greatest of Minoan shrines, the Archaeological Museum in Iraklion.

Work in other art-forms also proliferated. Jewellery of the 'Old Palace' period is wonderfully intricate and clear. Sealstone carving continued to develop. Metalwork generally, and the production of weapons in particular, reached an exceedingly high standard. In shrines on mountain peaks and deep in caves, worshippers of the Minoan deities left behind vigorous and delightful miniature sculptures.

While all this great profusion was at its height, at about 1700BC, all the palaces were destroyed to their foundations, apparently all at once and most probably by earthquake. But almost at once the Minoans were able to pick themselves up and to construct a fresh set of palaces, even larger and more elaborate than their predecessors, on the same sites. These are the 'New' Palaces, mighty buildings whose ruins can still be seen today at Knossos and Phaistos and in slightly more modest form at Malia and Kato Zakros. With their construction, architecture now steps to the fore as the leading art-form. Some of the palaces were on several storeys, with theatrical-looking steps and performance areas outside, great staircases mounting within and characteristic inverted pillars, thicker at the top than at the bottom. Walls were lined with the finest materials and decorated with the frescoes which are a familiar trademark of the Minoans. Even in ruins, the great palaces are extraordinary and evocative places, but they are also baffling and can be disconcerting. Maybe this is simply because they *are* ruins and difficult to interpret, but it is conceivable that they are not what they seem. The accepted view is that the palaces were the homes of the Minoan ruling class, probably one, or possibly several, royal families. The palaces formed the pivot of state and religious life, and were where the famous bull-leaping ceremonies took place; in short, they were full of life and richness. But there is another view, and it is that these were actually

The exuberance of a ceremony held thousands of years ago is captured in a bull-leaping fresco in Iraklion's Archaeological Museum

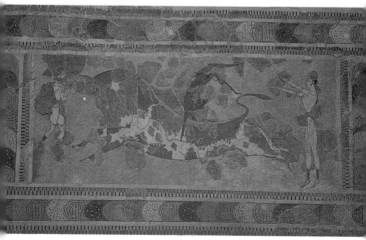

palaces of the dead, inhabited only by those performing the rites that would satisfy the gods, or the spirits of the dead. Classical archaeologists reject the theory, but it has precedents in Egyptian tombs, for example, and Neolithic burial places elsewhere in Europe. No one knows, and there are many who would rather not know.

About the spiritual and social workings of Minoan civilisation, precious little is known—even from seemingly straightforward objects. The Minoan bull is ever-present and must have represented some aspect of divinity—perhaps the earth and earthquakes; the leading divinity seems to have been a goddess, mistress of the animals, close to the heart of nature.

Women in Minoan palace society appear to have had a high position. So many works of art are to do with sports or pleasure that it has often been argued that this must also have been an unusually playful society, at peace with itself as well as with its neighbours. It is clear that Crete was an important trading nation, and probably an important maritime power. Certainly, this is what later Greek historians like Thucydides believed.

As for ordinary people, it is likely that they lived in a very simple way in crowded towns. The population of Minoan Crete may have been very large. We do not know how society was governed or what the relationship was between palaces and towns. There is a distinct impression of two levels of society with a wide division between them. We can say with certainty that those involved in the palace society lived in the presence of some of the most beautiful art objects ever made.

All this came to an end, through most of Crete, in about 1450BC, when the 'New' Palaces were two and a half centuries old. Kato Zakros, Malia and Phaistos were destroyed. Knossos was partly destroyed, was then repaired and staggered on for perhaps another 70 years. What happened has been a matter of the keenest conjecture. The original theory was that the palaces had been destroyed by attackers, perhaps the Achaians (or Acheans) also known as Myceneans, mainland Greeks from the north. These are the people of whom buried memories persist in the

At Knossos, parts of the New Palace have survived for over 3,000 years; its predecessor was razed to the ground

epics of Homer, which were composed centuries later and written down centuries later again. But it was also known that the island of Santorini north of Crete, itself a Minoan colony, had been destroyed by a mighty volcanic eruption at about that time. So the second theory of the destruction of the palaces pinned the blame on Santorini. The current belief among archaeologists is that the Santorini eruption occurred 50 years earlier than the catastrophe and that the fall of Minoan Crete was indeed the responsibility of attackers.

This theory seems to be supported by evidence drawn from language and writing. A script in linear form (known as Linear A) was developed quite early on during the Minoan period and was used to write in a language which has not yet been read. A new language came in at about the end of the New Palace period (written in hieroglyphics called Linear B) with many

inscriptions surviving on tablets. After much
scholarly argument, it has now been accepted
that the language written in Linear B was an
early form of Greek. This makes it virtually
certain that a Greek-speaking people was
dominant in Knossos during its final years.
Certainly we know from Greek myth of the
central importance of Crete to the ancient
Greeks both as a home of the gods and the home
of Minos and the Minotaur.

Crete in Myth

For the ancient Greeks, whose civilisation
reached its height 1,000 years after the collapse
of the Minoan, there were essentially two sets of
myths about Crete. One concerned Zeus, the
leading figure in the Greek pantheon. The belief
that associated him so strongly with Crete made
the island a holy place for the Greeks. The other
set of myths concerned Minos, and may have
contained, however deeply buried, some
fragments of a genuine tradition passed on by
the Achaians.

Zeus was generally believed in the ancient
world to have been born in a cave on Crete, the
son of Rhea and the monstrous figure Kronos.
There was also a Cretan belief that Zeus was
dead and buried on Mt Youktas, a peak just
behind Iraklion. From a certain angle Youktas
has an uncanny look of a helmeted warrior. A
number of other Greek gods and goddesses are
associated with Crete and there are hosts of
secondary figures. One of the most interesting is
the bronze giant Talos who ran continually round
the coast destroying those who attempted to
land there. In some versions, he was finally
betrayed and killed by Medea, sorceress and
wife of Jason, as she and Jason and the other
Argonauts returned to Greece at the end of their
quest for the Golden Fleece.

Stories of Minos tell of two brothers – Minos and
Rhadmanthys, both kings and lawgivers. Minos
ruled in Knossos, Rhadmanthys perhaps in
Phaistos. Every nine years Minos went to a
sacred cave and met Zeus face to face. His wife,
Pasiphae, fell in love with a bull, and their
offspring was a beast called the Minotaur, so
terrible that he had to be confined in a labyrinth
at Knossos, purpose-built by the great engineer

Daidalos (Daedalus). Young men and women were brought each year from Athens to be devoured by the Minotaur, until Theseus, son of King Aegeus, joined the prospective victims and killed the beast. The story goes that upon his arrival at Knossos, Minos's daughter Ariadne fell in love with the Athenian prince. She gave him a ball of thread which he unwound behind him as he made his way through the labyrinth to the Minotaur's lair. By following the thread, Theseus escaped and fled with Ariadne, though he later abandoned her on the island of Naxos. Then he and his companions sailed for Athens. The plan was that they should hoist a white sail in place of black as a signal of success. (Black would mean that Theseus was dead.) But they forgot to make the change and King Aegeus, mistakenly believing his son to be dead, threw himself into the sea when he saw the black sail approaching. Since then the sea has been called the Aegean in his honour.

Daidalos the engineer had helped Ariadne in the plot against the Minotaur and he too had to

Jason and the Argonauts are guided through the night by Tiphys. Jason's wife Medea was said to have killed Crete's bronze giant Talos

flee from Crete. He constructed two sets of wings, with feathers held in place by wax. One was for himself, one for his son Ikaros (Icarus). Daidalos flew successfully, but Ikaros flew too close to the sun—with fatal consequences. The wax melted and he plunged into the sea. Minos, when he died, went down to the underworld and took up duties there as lawgiver to the dead.

There are many references to Crete in the *Odyssey* and the *Iliad*, attributed to the blind poet Homer and dating from about 900BC. He tells of a powerful king named Idomeneos, grandson of Minos, who took a Cretan fleet to the Trojan wars. Homer's stories and place-names, so it appears today, are derived from oral tradition based on the Myceneans or Achaians who inhabited mainland Greece from the time of the late Minoans and flourished for several centuries after that. These, of course, were the very people who had probably conquered Minoan Crete. He refers to Crete as 'fair and fertile' and mentions 90 cities, some of them by name. He also refers to an indigenous Cretan people who may have been the last of the Minoans, living on under Mycenean rule.

Crete in History

The Myceneans/Achaians, who were the dominant force at the end of the Minoan period, were replaced by a new set of Greek-speaking arrivals, the Dorians from the north. They built stout citadels, many of which survive as impressive ruins. They also made handsome, simple sculpture of a kind called Daidalic— immensely important in helping to start up the sculptural tradition of classical Greece—and organised themselves into small city-states in a way that prefigured the classical Greek world. They were extremely conservative by temperament and may have passed on their own form of social organisation to Sparta in the Peloponnese.

Next came the Romans, who took over the island in 67BC after three years of bitter campaigning. The Roman period in Crete, which lasted four centuries, was prosperous and settled. Then, from the late 4th century, when Constantine moved the capital of the empire to

The Byzantine influence in Crete outlasted Byzantine rule, and was strikingly expressed in chapel frescoes such as this one in Kritsa

Constantinople (modern Istanbul), Crete, by now Christian, came under eastern influence. It remained in the Byzantine world for most of 900 years—with one extremely significant interruption.

In AD824 Crete was captured and occupied by Arab raiders, who destroyed the Roman basilicas and a good deal else besides. In 961 the Byzantines, led by the future emperor Nikephoras Phokas, retook the island amid scenes of the greatest violence. Nikephoras Phokas is remembered today in street names in many Cretan towns. Under the Byzantine rule which ensued, art-forms manifested themselves most beautifully with the construction of rural chapels, decorated with frescoes. The frescoes showed God the ruler of all, known as the Pantocrator; Jesus, Mary and the saints; and a host of stories from the Christian canon, all in a ritualised arrangement and in the strange

BACKGROUND

hierarchical perspective of the Byzantines. This strong tradition was maintained for centuries, long after Byzantine rule had ended. Only a few frescoes have been restored but they remain an important and sometimes moving aspect of an exploration of Crete.

After the sack of Constantinople in 1204, dominance in Crete passed first to the Genoese and then to the Venetian empire. The Venetians took timber from the island, accelerating a process of deforestation which finally wiped out almost all the cypress forests for which the island had been famous. For the Cretans themselves, the long Venetian period (1210 to 1669) was a hard and bitter time. They were virtually slaves, ferociously repressed and often in rebellion.

The Venetians built strong defences in the major towns and a number of fine castles all round the island, both to repel invaders and to quell the populace. Though often ruined, almost all of these survive and are one of the great features of the island.

During long wars in the mid-17th century, the

Crete's history has been one of foreign rule and rebellion. In the 19th century there were many uprisings against the Turkish rulers

Turks captured most of the island and Iraklion itself—known then as El Khandak or Candia—was finally taken in 1669 after a 20-year siege. This ushered in the most desperate period of Cretan history. Turkish rule was arbitrary and capricious. There were many revolts, most notably that of Ioannis Daskaloyiannis in 1770. Many Cretans converted to Islam. During the 19th century as the Greek independence movement gained strength on the mainland, the Cretans indulged in their own rebellions, and the long revolutionary tradition of the island was strengthened at immeasurable cost in blood and destruction.

Peace lasted until 1922, when following Greece's defeat in a war against Turkey, Greeks living on the west coast of Turkey were exchanged for Turks still resident in Greece. This transfer of populations has given Crete the homogeneous Greek character which distinguishes it so sharply from Cyprus.

In World War II Crete was once more a place of bitter struggle. The Italians entered Albania and were held there by the Greeks. Then the Germans came into the contest, rolling up not just the Greek army but also the Allied expeditionary force that had been sent to the Greek mainland. Both forces, Greek and Allied, now retreated to Crete and joined the Allied garrison holding the island. Within a pitifully brief period the Germans had caught up with them again and the Battle of Crete began.

It lasted barely a week. The island's defences were poorly organised. German dominance of the air was total, and British naval ships from Egypt could not get into the crucial northern ports without exposing themselves to air attack. On May 20, 1941, German gliders and paratroops swooped on all the airfields of the north coast—Iraklion, Rethimnon and Maleme in the west. They were held in Iraklion and Rethimnon but in Maleme they opened up a chink and little by little forced their way out through it to turn the Allied retreat into a rout. The battle had been a terrible one and now the Allies staged a fearful march across the mountains to be taken off from the southern coast by British ships. The Greeks, who had fought heroically, were simply abandoned and so,

BACKGROUND

finally, were 5,000 Allied troops when the navy could no longer get in to the little port of Hora Sfakion where they were trapped. These men were either captured or sheltered by Cretans and many later managed to escape. That any of them had even got as far as Sfakia, was due to a Greek regiment on the far side of the mountains which held the German forces and provided an escape route. During the Battle of Crete many bands of freelance warriors sprang into existence and these, together with Allied operatives later put ashore on Crete, now formed the nucleus of increasingly determined and well-organised resistance.

Tales of Cretan heroism between 1941 and the war's end are legion, and in one stunning propaganda coup the German general on Crete was captured and spirited off the island by the well-organised resistance—an event celebrated in the famous film *Ill Met by Moonlight*.

After the war, Crete was extremely poor and life returned to normality only very slowly. Many of the young men were obliged to leave in search of work. By the 1960s, however, tourism began to make an impact. Changes have since been very swift and much of the development is unplanned and lacks cohesion. It is visibly the case, however, that many tourist enterprises are small enough and local enough for the benefits to have spread out surprisingly widely. In the light of Crete's bitter modern history, it is hard to resent the island's current good fortune. At the same time, one cannot fail to notice the contrast between the tourist strip on some parts of the northern coast and the achievements of the Minoans thousands of years before.

Although the modern Greek state originated in 1832, Crete remained firmly in Turkish hands till the end of the century. It came briefly under joint rule by Russia, France, Britain and Italy, and until recently it was possible to meet old people in Rethimnon who remembered Russian occupation of their town. Finally, the murder in Iraklion of 14 British soldiers and the British consul brought Turkish rule to an end. But it was not until 1913, and after further bitter political struggles, that Crete officially became part of Greece.

IRAKLION AND
CENTRAL CRETE

Ayios Nikolaos, away to the east, is the most populous individual resort in Crete, and Khania in the west impresses many as the finest. But Iraklion and its large district, right in the centre, are cumulatively the most visited. Iraklion itself is by far the largest town on the island. Knossos, the main Minoan site, is near by; and the Archaeological Museum, gathering the best from all the Minoan sites in Crete, is in town. Except for the Archaeological Museum in Athens, this is the largest and finest in Greece— and, of course, it has the finest Minoan collection anywhere. Phaistos, the most important

Ayia Ekaterini church nestles beside the 19th-century cathedral

Minoan palace after Knossos, is in the southern part of central Crete, flanked by the lovely Minoan site at Ayia Triada and by later, extensive ruins at Gortyn. All of these places are in the rich Plain of Mesara, overlooked by the bulk of Mount Psiloritis.
Iraklion is not a resort. Most visitors to the centre stay in hotels along the beaches of the north coast, specially in Hersonisos and Malia. Rather fewer stay in the central south, though the fine beaches and man-made caves of Matala have attracted fame of a sort, and Ayia Galini, a crowded little resort on the south coast, is not far distant in the prefecture of Rethimnon.

IRAKLION

Those who are accustomed to Middle Eastern towns will not be

IRÁKLION

Sea of Crete

Venetian Fortress

Venetian Harbour

VENIZELOU

St. Andrew's Bastion

City Walls

VENIZELOU

MAKARIOU

Historical Museum

EPIMENIDOU

St. Titus Church

El Greco Park

HANDAKOS

GIAMALAKI

City Hall

St. Marks Church

VENIZELOU SQUARE

MALIKOUTI

Sabbionera Bastion

Archaeological Museum

Morosini Fountain

Ayia Ekaterini

KALOKERINOU

NIKIFOROS PHOKAS SQUARE

DAEDALOU

Tourist Information Office

DIKEOSINIS

ELEFTHERIAS SQUARE

Pantokrator Bastion

Khania Gate

Cathedral

AYIA MINA

MONIS KARDIOTISSIS

Market

ODOS 1821

ODOS 1866

Post Office

EVANS

IKAROU

Vitouri Bastion

City Walls

MARTIRON

PLASTIRA

KORNAROU SQUARE

AVEROF OINONOS

EVANS

DIMOKRITIS

THERISOU

Bethlehem Bastion

ROMANOU

Bethlehem Gate

PLASTIRA

Kenouria Gate

Kazantzakis Tomb

Jesus Bastion

KONDILAKI

Martinengo Bastion

KNOSOU

AKADIMIAS

To Knossos

0   200   400 metres

To Rethimnon & Phaistos

To Airport & Ayios Nikolaos

surprised by Iraklion, fifth city of Greece, and undisputed centre of Cretan life. It is a place of concrete and flat roofs, a noisy, sprawling, dusty, active, 20th-century kind of city, not at all what one might expect as point of entry to an island of sea and beaches, snow-white chapels and the extraordinary wealth of antiquities which helps to make Crete a place apart. Yet there Iraklion stands, right in the middle, with the island's principal port at its heart and the island's main airport just out to the east.

It is almost impossible to avoid the city while visiting Crete. Many are drawn by the Archaeological Museum, the world's main showplace for Minoan artefacts; or they pass through to visit the neighbouring Minoan site of Knossos. Backpackers and other visitors off the ferries, however, may well spend a night or two here before moving on, and the city's rather mediocre lodging houses are crammed in summer. But, however they come and however long they stay, almost all visitors are mildly shocked at first by Iraklion. Although it is per capita the wealthiest city in Greece, it seems impossibly drab and dingy.

There is, however, a surprising amount to see. Crete's greatest concentration of professional people may be seen at work and play in and around Iraklion. Villagers come in from a wide area to sell their produce, buy provisions or deal with money matters. The city seems almost relaxed, certainly at its most genial, at the hour of the *volta*, the communal evening stroll. The central part of Iraklion is a walled town with massive Venetian ramparts generally invisible among houses or other obstructions. Visitors entering the city from any landward point must somehow pierce the ramparts to reach the middle. There are handsome and massive Venetian gates in the west (the Khania Gate) and in the south (the 'new' or Kenouria Gate), through which passes Odos Evans (Evans Street), a name famous in archaeology (see **Knossos**, below). Those arriving from the east, from Ayios Nikolaos or the airport, will follow the main road through miles of dreary outskirts, then suddenly ascend a steep bend through the ramparts to find themselves in a semi-circular 'square', leafy but traffic-ridden, ringed on the far side with cafés and restaurants. This is the **Plateia Eleftherias**, or Freedom Square, a gathering point from which the city radiates westwards. In one corner stands the Archaeological Museum with the main Tourist Information Office opposite.

From the Plateia Eleftherias, the Odos Dhikeosinis (Dikheosinis Street) leads to the square named for the Byzantine emperor Nikephoras Phokas. This is the true centre of town. If you now face the sea, directly behind you is the main market of Iraklion, in a crowded little street named Odos 1866.

Directly in front, a bigger street leads to the old harbour, with long harbour mole and vast and somewhat blank Venetian fortress. To your left from Nikephoras Phokas, the main road winds away towards the Khania Gate.

The **market of Iraklion** is a fine little scrimmage of a place, with vegetables and herbs and sponges, clasp knives, shoes and sausages, a seemingly casual collection of all kinds of bits and pieces, representing many aspects of island life. It is hot and somewhat exhausting in summer but cheerful and energetic at all times of year. Up past the market the **Plateia Kornarou** (Kornarou Square) has a large statue of Eroktokritos and Arethousa, hero and heroine of a massive 17th-century epic poem by one Vincenzos Kornaros—for whom the square is named. Kornaros was from Sitia in the east and his

The liveliest place in Iraklion: its bustling market, where you can buy virtually anything

poem *The Erotokritos* is a
symbol of identity for Cretans
and many other Greeks, the
equivalent of a cross between
Shakespeare and *Rule Britannia*
for the British. There is also a fine
fountain in the square.
Returning to Nikephoras Phokas
and turning left along
Kalokerinou, the main road
leading towards the Khania
Gate, then left again quite
shortly, one reaches an open
space bounded on the far side
by the city's large 19th-century
cathedral—not a thing of
particular beauty. But this space
also contains the Sinaiite church
of St Katherine, **Ayia Ekaterini**,
with its fine collection of
paintings (see **What to See**,
below).
To the north from Nikephoras
Phokas is the road towards the
harbour. The open space almost
immediately entered, replete
with restaurants, fountain, pie
shop and newsagent, is
technically named the **Plateia
Venizelou** (Square of Venizelos)
after the Cretan-born statesman
who was Greek prime minister
for many years and ushered
Crete into the modern nation in
1913. Foreigners know it as
'Fountain Square'. The 'Morosini
Fountain' at its centre is
Venetian, built in 1628 but
incorporating a set of delightfully
worn-out 14th-century lions.
Almost immediately, to the right,
is a reconstructed Venetian
church, St Mark's. This is
followed very shortly by the
reconstructed Venetian Loggia
now used as the city hall. Tucked
in behind, in a pretty little open
space, is the church of St Titus.
The main road, Odos Avgoustou

25 (August 25 Street) now
leads on down towards the port,
passing El Greco Park. The
Cretan painter Domenico
Theotokopoulos, 1541–1614,
moved from Iraklion to Italy in
his 20s and finally to Spain where
he was known, of course, as El
Greco, 'the Greek'.
After a short walk, August 25
debouches on the old harbour,
with the fortress opposite.

WHAT TO SEE

◆◆◆
ARCHAEOLOGICAL MUSEUM
Eleftherias Square
This is undoubtedly the star
attraction of Iraklion, despite its
ageing, shoddy building and
surging summer crowds. In the
days before mass seaside
holidays, this museum, along
with the palaces of Knossos and
Phaistos, was considered the
main reason for visiting Crete. It
still remains central to the
pleasure and understanding of
many visitors.
It is best to go early or at
lunchtime, in the hope of beating
the worst of the crush; and best
of all to go twice. After some
palace visiting, it is doubly
rewarding to return to the
museum for a slow perusal,
matching a growing sense of
Minoan art, architecture and
stylistic change against the
known flow of events.
The display is set out in rough
chronological order from
galleries I to XII, covering the
ground from Neolithic and early
Minoan, right through the height
of the Minoan period and then
out again into the post-palatial
and Dorian era. A major gallery

of Minoan sarcophagi is followed by a centrally important exhibition of Minoan frescoes, and, when it is open, by a fine collection of Minoan artefacts assembled by a private individual, one Dr Giamalakis. After this the museum again picks up the chronological story, the final rooms covering Greek and Roman antiquity.

It is astonishing how rich and prolific the earliest Minoan periods were (mainly in gallery 1). There were several distinctive pottery types. Vassiliki ware is the most interesting, usually jugs with

A late Minoan pot decorated with papyrus flowers

overlong spouts and an odd 'flamed' effect where the clay has been mottled by uneven application of fire, perhaps with a burning bunch of twigs. There are beautiful stone jars and intriguing stone boxes. Two of these, one a complete box and one merely a lid, show long leggy dogs sprawled across their surfaces, a high point of Minoan naturalism. This gallery also contains a fascinating range of jewellery and sealstones, two areas of production in which the

Minoans were to excel throughout their civilisation. Galleries II and III cover the Old Palace Period, initially with more Vassiliki ware and small-scale sculptures from peak shrines (the Minoans were true miniaturists when it came to sculpture). There are also faience plaques depicting Minoan houses. The dominant pottery is now described as Kamares ware, much of it from Phaistos and the Phaistos area. Some Kamares vessels are perilously thin, and known accordingly as egg-shell ware. The Phaistos Disk is also exhibited here. This is a clay disk stamped in a spiral with hieroglyphics still impenetrable to scholars. It is sometimes

Iraklion Museum: Minoan clay figurines sometimes referred to as 'poppy goddesses'

claimed, at least half seriously, as an early example of printing. Gallery IV is packed with Minoan artefacts of which some are magnificent and others tender and personal. It contains two tiny statues of priestesses, or perhaps goddesses, from the most sacred area of Knossos. One, with breasts bared, holds out snakes; the other, also bare-breasted, is liberally entwined with snakes. Here one may see the most famous Minoan bull's head, made of serpentine and with one surviving eye in jasper and rock crystal. It was probably a ritual container, called a *rhyton*, used for pouring out libations. A tiny ivory acrobat, caught in mid-air leap, shows how brilliantly Minoan artists could catch and convey movement and even portray such naturalistic detail as veins

along an arm. There is a sword (from Malia) almost 3ft (1m) long and a gold sword pommel, in the form of a disk with a hole in its centre. Another athlete is shown on the disk, bent right round backwards so that his feet rest on his head. Pottery masterpieces include a ravishing jug, covered all over with a pattern of reeds.

The museum contains many double-headed axes, either real or depicted on vast pottery storage jars. These axes were ornamental or symbolic, not for chopping or fighting. In Greek the word for double-axe is *labrys*. Because the double-axe is omnipresent, it seems quite plausible that the word *labrys* was transmuted into *labyrinth* and used as the name for the palace of Knossos itself. This was a name which survived, of course, and with great potency, into later Greek myth and almost every modern European language.

During the later periods, there were wonderful pottery vessels, often large, covered with writhing, flowing marine forms, the sad-eyed octopus the most impressive among them. From Ayia Triada (see page 31) come three carved conical rhytons, one showing boxing, one supposedly a chieftain receiving a tribute of hides, the third a procession of merrymakers. This latter, known as the Harvester Vase, is sometimes regarded as the finest low relief carving discovered anywhere in the Mediterranean basin. The Minoan sarcophagi in gallery XIII are a great surprise—bath-tubs used for burials and big clay chests called *larnakes*. The frescoes just upstairs are marvellous, even though much ruined and much restored, often conjecturally. It is well to conserve some energy for them. The older ones are smaller than those made at the height of the New Palace period. They include a figure dubbed 'la Parisienne' at the time of her excavation. The face, with its huge eye and bumpy nose, the neck flowing with ringlets and with a sacred knot tied just behind, are remarkably vivid. There is the larger and newer 'Prince of the Lilies' with his plumed head-dress, a reconstruction which scholars have come to doubt, thinking now the original may have shown several figures. One of the most important exhibits in this room, indeed in the whole museum, is a painted sarcophagus from Ayia Triada. It is made of stone, and covered in painted plaster. This beautiful object clearly shows religious ceremonial in progress. In this gallery there is also the largest of the bull-leaping frescoes, from Knossos, showing a male athlete, in mid-somersault. At the same moment a woman athlete begins her leap and another stands behind the bull to catch and steady the leapers.

The final rooms, devoted to the Minoans' successors, may come as something of an anticlimax; but they contain sculptures of great importance to the development of Greek art, and a set of bronze shields of exceptional beauty and significance. To appreciate these it may even be necessary to make a third visit.

AYIA EKATERINI
Plateia Ayia Ekaterini
This simple 15th-century church with a later Venetian doorway houses various fine works of Cretan religious art. The most beautiful are the paintings of Mikalis Damaskinos. Like his contemporary El Greco, Damaskinos also went to Italy, returning late in his life to Crete and here little by little re-adopting the 'Byzantine' ways of painting he had previously discarded. See particularly *The Divine Liturgy* and *The First Ecumenical Council (1591)*, an unpromising-sounding subject for a marvellous painting.

HISTORICAL MUSEUM
opposite the Xenia hotel, west of the old harbour
This is more of a treat than many of its kind, containing displays that help to give some idea of Cretan life as well as Crete's tumultuous history. On the ground floor, there are portraits, weapons and other memorials of Cretan resistance fighters from Turkish times, the 'captains' or *palikares* whose deeds are also celebrated in monastery and schoolroom displays elsewhere in the island. There are religious objects, many from early days at St Titus in Gortyn and some notable icons (particularly pleasurable is the Zoodokos Pygi or 'Life-Giving Well'). The upper floors house a replica of the study of Cretan writer Nikos Kazantzakis (1883–1957, author of *Freedom and Death, Zorba the Greek*, etc) and celebrate Emmanuel Tsouderos, the Cretan who was Greek prime minister—and in refuge on Crete—during the battle for the island in 1941. He escaped over the White Mountains from Khania with King George of the Hellenes and was taken off by boat from the mouth of the Samaria Gorge. There is also an excellent collection of Cretan textiles and rural furniture and furnishings. This helps to enrich visits to villages in the Cretan countryside and is a particularly good preliminary for trips to the popular weaving centres of Anoyia and Kritsa.

At various points in the museum there are illuminating photographic displays and in the basement a rich collection of architectural details and fragments.

KAZANTZAKIS TOMB
Martinengo Bastion
The epitaph for Kazantzakis's simple grave is taken from his own works: 'I hope for nothing; I fear nothing; I am free'. The tomb is set at the southern extreme of the Venetian walls.

VENETIAN FORTRESS
This large building, reconstructed in 1523, has been tidied and depersonalised in the process of contemporary restoration. But it is still impressive, with good views from the battlements and sundry Lions of St Mark, the symbol of Venetian rule, carved in relief. This is the fortress that withstood

Crete's fortresses are a grim reminder of 400 years of Venetian rule

the Turkish siege of 20 years and was finally surrendered by Francesco Morosini the younger in 1669. The siege was the last great stand of Christendom in the eastern Mediterranean. During the Battle for Crete in World War II the last Allied defenders of Iraklion fought their way along the mole and escaped by boat to waiting ships. The castle is open in summer only. The Venetian fortress is at the end of the harbour mole.

Accommodation

The traditional stopping-over place in Iraklion for the moderately well-heeled was for many years the A-class **Astoria** (tel: 081 229012). This hotel is right in Eleftherias Square, within whispering distance of the Archaeological Museum. Some of the rooms, especially on the upper floors, give pleasant views over the square; and though it may seem a little old-fashioned

today, it remains popular and with friendly service. One or two more modern hotels have sprung up recently and some even offer swimming pools, most desirable in counteracting the hot and very 'towny' feel of Iraklion. The **Galaxy** (A-class) in Dimokritias Street (tel: 081 238812) is one of the most promising, its rooms ranged round a central court with pool. Its bar is popular with local people – another advantage. But it is a good step further from the centre than the Astoria. Down towards the lower end of the scale, but friendly and cheerful as well as being much cheaper, is the **Daedalos**, C-class (tel: 081 224391). Its situation in pedestrian Daedalou Street, perhaps 100 yards (100m) from the Astoria, is central and lively.

Nightlife

There are discos here, but Iraklion is not a centre for this kind of nightlife. Better to try Cretan music—the plangent, three-stringed Cretan lyre figures large at **Kastro** and **Delina**, on the way to the airport, convenient by taxi. There are bouzouki places out of town, among them the **Ariadne** at Knossos. These are noisy and can be expensive.

Restaurants

Iraklion is not a wonderful place for eating; indeed, its reputation is decidedly poor. But it is a good place for that fine Greek pastime—sitting out at a café table for a slow beer or coffee. There are numerous outdoor restaurants in Venizelou Square and also, on the north side, a small shop selling good cheese pies (*tiropitta*) and *bougatsa*, a sweet cheese pie with cinnamon. There are also many restaurants, including a Chinese, in the narrow pedestrian street, Daedalou, leading from

Leisurely meals: a Cretan tradition

Venizelou Square back towards Elleftherias Square and parallel with the main road. The **Rover Pub** here is popular with tourists for its unthreatening cleanliness. **Kosta's**, at number 6, has a fair menu. In a small alley leading between the market and Odos Evans there is another press of restaurants, more ethnic and perhaps requiring a little daring for first-time visitors. These were originally the simplest of market restaurants serving great bowls of beans to villagers. Now they have turned to summer visitors as well and serve meat roast on the spit and over charcoal grills. Check prices first. There are also a few smarter restaurants, patronised by middle-class Greeks. **Kiriakos**, in Dimokritias Street, three minutes outside the city walls from Eleftherias Square, is an example.

Shopping

The market is the place for fruit, vegetables and oddments. Iraklion also has a full range of basic shops, many in Kalokairinou, the stretch of main road between Nikephoras Phokas and the Khania Gate. These are not remarkable. Smart boutiques, their presence an astonishment to those who have known Crete over the years, feature in Daedalou Street. There is a Christian Dior here, for instance, and Budari, a smart Italian shoe and leather shop. Sofos sells well-designed women's clothes and G. Frangidakis shows some good quality Cretan jewellery. Iraklion also has antique shops, though not all inspire confidence; try August 25th Street.

Ayia Triada has thrown up more questions than answers about Minoan life

WHAT TO SEE IN CENTRAL CRETE

AYIA TRIADA (AYÍA TRIADHA)

This set of ruins, excavated by the Italians and named after a nearby church (the Holy Trinity), occupies a site even lovelier than that of Phaistos (see below). On the western end of a hill, it looks across the final stretch of the Mesara towards the sea— which, in Minoan times, quite probably came right up to the foot of the hill. The mouth of the Kamares Cave on Psiloritis is also visible from here.

In general terms, Ayia Triada is a puzzle. What was the purpose of a set of secondary palatial buildings so close to the great palaces of Phaistos? It has often been described as a summer palace; some believe it may have been used as a principal residence after the destruction of Phaistos; and there is also a suggestion that it may itself have been composed of two different establishments.

For the non-technically minded visitor, the pleasure in this considerably less-visited site will probably lie mainly in its position and in the knowledge that many of the most beautiful of all Minoan works of art were found here. There was also a small township immediately adjacent, which included what looks remarkably like a row of shops.

The conventional way to see the site is first to pay a visit to the small Byzantine chapel—Ayios Yeoryios Galatas, with 14th-century frescoes—on a small hill opposite and slightly to the left. From here it becomes apparent that the palatial or semi palatial buildings formed an L-shape. The splendid conical *rhyton* called the Chieftain's Cup was found among the small rooms just to the south (Archaeological Museum, Iraklion, gallery VII). There are a number of important rooms at the junction of the 'L', including one referred to as a hall, one with benches round its walls and restored gypsum cladding, and a third with a raised slab of gypsum in the floor. This may have served as a platform for a wooden bed. That great masterpiece the Harvester Vase was found in this corner of the site, along with the 'Boxer Rhyton'. They appear to have fallen through from the floor above—and smashed to pieces—at the time of the destruction of the building. In this area major frescoes were discovered, including a marvellous scene of a cat hunting a pheasant ⬎ (Archaeological Museum, gallery XIV). A little up right from these rooms, under a protective roof, there are chambers and magazines belonging to the main building. In Achaian times, a further palace appears to have been built on top. Outside, on the west side, run the remnants of a Minoan road.

The town and its shops, a dense, packed zone partly from the post-palace, Mycenean period lie further up, bending northwards towards Psiloritis to form a second L shape. The shops are in a row on the right-hand (eastern) side of the site. The beautiful and important Ayia Triada sarcophagus was found about 500ft (150m) further east (Archaeological Museum, Iraklion gallery XIII).

Ayia Triada is 2 miles (3km) west of Phaistos.

◆◆
GORTYN

Sometimes known as Gortys (in direct transcription from Greek), this large and sprawling site is Dorian, Roman and early Byzantine. It has never been fully excavated and visitors may well find interesting ruins by wandering outside the peripheral fence. The most significant parts of the site, however, are enclosed within the fence.

It was on the banks of the river here in Gortyn, so the Greeks believed, that Zeus seduced Europa, having taken the form of a bull, and brought her to Crete on his back. Europa, of course, has given her name to a continent. Historically speaking, the town rose to prominence only at the end of the Minoan era. It soon became an important city-state.

For us today, and especially for those interested in the law, Gortyn has a unique importance. Found among the later ruins—in which they had been incorporated as useful building materials—were a number of large, inscribed stone blocks.

Reassembled and deciphered, these proved to contain the first known code of law in Europe, dating from the 5th century BC. The laws of Gortyn are extremely hierarchical and match what is known of the conservatism and militarism of Dorian Crete. They deal, among other things, with property in marriage, and with adultery and rape. The code, which reads from left to right and then from right to left again, each line starting where the one before it ended, is beautifully incised.

The other most important pre-Roman remnant at Gortyn is the temple of **Apollo Pythios**, on the far side of the road. There is an altar and sundry bits of broken column.

Roman Gortyn, which came next,

Stones at Gortyn: the ruins date from Dorian to Byzantine times

was huge, with perhaps about 300,000 people. Unlike Knossos, it had sided with the Roman invaders in 65BC and as a result was not destroyed. Instead, it became the capital of a province, controlling large areas of North Africa, and it possessed many impressive public buildings. The best preserved of these—just near the re-erected Code—is the **Odeum** (1st century AD). This was a roofed building used for theatrical and other performances; there are fairly substantial stone and brick remains.

Possibly the most interesting building of all, however, is the early Christian **Basilica of St Titus**. Titus was sent to Crete by St Paul, who had himself had some adventures in the island. It was also Paul, in an epistle to Titus, who spoke of Cretans as 'liars, evil beasts, slow bellies'.

Titus himself was martyred in Gortyn; the basilica supposedly marks the spot. It was a large building with triple nave and dome, bringing elements from Byzantium to an essentially Roman formula. A large and dignified section of the apse and its surrounds is still standing. Gortyn was sacked by Arab raiders in 825AD and never rebuilt. But the Italian monk Buondelmonte, travelling in Crete in the 15th century, described its ruins as 'equal in grandeur to our own Florence'. The road leads on through Mires, a busy but rather ugly agricultural centre with numerous small restaurants, rooms to rent, and cafés for a cooling drink. It has a surprisingly energetic street life. A side-road to the south leads to Matala. Shortly beyond Mires, just off the main road, lie Phaistos and Ayia Triada.

Gortyn is 30 miles (48km) south of Iraklion on the main road to Phaistos.

◆
HERSONISOS (KHERSÓNISOS)

This is the first real resort as one travels eastward from Iraklion on the northern coastal plain. Technically its name is Limani Hersonisos—Port of Hersonisos. It is listed under 'L' in alphabetical publications (telephone book, official tourist literature, etc). Hersonisos has underwater relics of an ancient port and fish tanks cut into rock on the far side of the little headland. But for the rest, it is a modern creation (the original village is up and a little inland). The fast main road runs straight through the town. Beaches are in short supply but the front is prettily thronged with restaurants.

Also on the front there are some surprisingly up-market boutiques, specialising in jewellery, leather and fur. Hersonisos is reached by taking the New Road east from Iraklion.

◆◆◆
KNOSSOS (KNOSÓS)

Knossos is popular and crowded for the best of reasons: it is an extraordinarily interesting place. What stands out immediately is the extent to which it has been reconstructed. Whether or not the reconstruction is acceptable, the site certainly gives a strong impression of how a Minoan palace *may* have looked and makes a subsequent visit to the other major palaces—Phaistos, Malia and Zakros—all the more rewarding.

The excavator and author of its reconstruction was the Englishman, Sir Arthur Evans. He began to dig just at the start of the 20th century at a time of high archaeological excitement. Over the previous 30 years or so the amateur archaeologist Heinrich Schliemann had been able to show, at Troy and sites on the Greek mainland, that there were substantial ruins at many of the places mentioned by Homer. These antedated classical Greece by centuries. Schliemann had in fact begun to reveal the existence and some of the treasures of what is now most often called the Achaian civilisation, also referred to as Mycenean. Schliemann had wanted to dig at Knossos but

KNOSSOS

Existing Wall
Conjectural Wall

1	Theatre Area	7	Grand Staircase
2	South Propylaeum	8	Hall of the Double Axes
3	Throne Room	9	Queen's Rooms
4	Pillar Crypts	10	Shrine of the Double Axes
5	Central Court	11	Court of the Stone Spout
6	Priest King Fresco	12	Pillar Hall

failed to buy the land. Arthur Evans eventually succeeded in acquiring the site, and years of major digs pushed back European prehistory by millennia, as they laid bare the bones of the foremost Minoan site. Evans reconstructed as he went, in order to preserve his findings against storm and potential earthquake.

With some small exceptions, what is visible on the site is the New Palace, built up after the disaster of 1700BC. The west wall is marked by the fire of its own final destruction. Pathways crossing the paved areas immediately surrounding the palace are slightly raised, producing a 'causeway' effect. Entry is generally through the west porch and then along the wiggling remnants of the so-called Corridor of the Procession, parts of which have slipped off the corner of the hill. In due course one reaches an extremely handsome, pillared southern entrance where replicas of some of the major frescoes are displayed (the originals are in the Iraklion Archaeological Museum, gallery XIV). The southern entrance leads to a large central court, a feature of all the principal Minoan palaces.

An even more dramatic entry can be made through the narrow north entrance, though as you approach it you will have to pass several points of interest better left to the end of a visit (some well-like storage pits and a 'theatral area'). The northern entrance-way, achieving its present form late on, featured a narrow and steeply rising ramp passing beneath a porch which bore the awesome bas relief of a bull (there is a replica in the proper position; the original is in the museum). This approach also leads into the central court. Here, on the westward side, there occurs a series of sacred chambers, dark and rather frightening. Deeper within is the throne room proper, where the throne, still on display, was found intact.

On the eastern side of the court lay what appears to have been the domestic quarter. There was an upper storey here, but also several more below, cut into the side of the steep hill and

Homer called Knossos 'a great city'; the palace ruins hint at past splendour

reached by a wide and gently
descending stairway bordered
by colonnade and light-well and
passing a series of fine rooms. Sir
Arthur Evans named this the
Grand Staircase and it is
generally regarded as one of the
most remarkable achievements
of prehistoric architecture.
Taking the stairway, the visitor
first encounters a large fresco
showing shields made of oxhide.
Descending again, and turning
to the right, one enters the Hall of
the Colonnades. This in turn
leads towards the so-called Hall
of the Double Axes, a name
derived from mason's marks in
the nearby light-well. It is also
known as the King's Megaron. It
was elaborately decorated and
divided by a polythyron (a
characteristically Minoan
arrangement of partition with
columns and door enabling a
room to be shut off from wind
and weather). Near by, reached
by a narrow dogleg passage, is
the room traditionally called the
Queen's Drawing Room or
Megaron. This fascinating room
has a fresco of dolphins (the
original is in Iraklion museum,
gallery XIV). Near by is another
chamber, bedroom or bathroom,
today containing a bath. There
was also a lavatory with drains to
carry away sewage.

As well as the most spectacular
parts of the palace, the 'theatral
area' on the northwest corner of
the complex is worth visiting.
This really is just like a little
outdoor theatre, with steps for a
seated or standing audience.
The Minoan road from the northwest leads straight up to it.
Knossos, 3 miles (5km) from
Iraklion, is reached by a road

leaving Eleftherias Square in a
southerly direction or, for those
coming along the coast, by a turn
off south from the New Road
without having to go into Iraklion.
Innumerable coach tours go to
Knossos from Iraklion, not to
mention the No 2 bus from
Eleftherias Square. It is also easy
to reach the site on day-trips
from other resorts and individual
hotels all along the north coast of
Crete.

◆◆
MALIA

Malia is one of the most extreme
examples of tourist jerry-
building in Crete, the brash and
gaudy style of the resort
contrasting sharply with the
peace and beauty of the Minoan
site a minute or two east by car.
As at Hersonisos, the main road
runs through town, with two
good restaurants, the Taverna
Plaka and the Melitos on either
side at the far end. From the
middle of the built-up area, a
smaller road leads down
towards the beach, so that shops,
restaurants and discos are
arranged on a T-shaped grid.
Down at the bottom of the road is
an excellent sandy beach which
naturally gets rather crowded.
Some have likened modern
Malia to a frontier town on the
Mexico/Texas border. But in all
fairness it is probably good fun if
you are under 18.
The Minoan palace of Malia,
one of the great four, lies just to
the seaward side of the main
road a mile (2km) beyond the
town. To the south in particular
there is a fine mountain
background, marking this as
another brilliant choice of

landscape by the Minoans. The ruins themselves, consisting as usual of fragments of the Old Palace and a lot more of the New, are relatively easy to understand, particularly if one is already a veteran of Knossos and Phaistos. There is the familiar arrangement around a central court—here a rather long and narrow one. The most sacred areas are to the west of the court and they are located close to storerooms. There are royal apartments, too, and as at the other palaces, part of the interest lies in seeing just where some of the most spectacular of the exhibits in the Iraklion Archaeological Museum were uncovered.

A raised causeway, typical of the Minoans, crosses the paved west court. At the southwest corner there is a series of circular storage pits, once roofed and most probably used for grain. Following the west flank and passing round the northwest corner, the visitor reaches the north court with giant storage jars (*pithoi*) on the left. To the right and slightly in front lie the 'royal apartments' with a lustral basin. The sword with acrobat curved round the pommel (Archaeological Museum, gallery IV), came from just west of here. On the nearer (northern) side of the Great Court was a pillared room, perhaps a kitchen with a dining room above, looking out over the court. As at Phaistos, the eastern side of the court was bounded by a colonnade in which stone piers alternated with upside-down wooden pillars. Various rooms behind this to the east are now roofed and locked.

The most exciting area is the west of the Great Courtyard. Here there was a pillar crypt, probably dark and awesome as at Knossos, with double axes scrawled into the pillars. A famous and much-illustrated axe-head in the shape of a leopard was found just near by, together with the great 'Malia sword' with rock crystal handle (both in gallery IV in the Archaeological Museum, Iraklion). The west side of the court had an upper storey and was undoubtedly imposing. At the southwest corner of the court is the most intriguing object of all, a round stone table with a depression at the centre and 34 smaller hollows round the edge.

Much ink has been spilled in trying to explain it.

Ten minutes' walk from the site, northeast towards the sea, was the Khrysolakkos or 'Gold Hole', a burial enclosure where the golden hornets of Malia and much other exquisite jewellery was found. It may also have been the source of the British Museum's so-called 'Aegina treasure'.

♦
MATALA
This growing resort has a warren of man-made caves. They were occupied by hippies during the 1960s and gave the village a special reputation, somewhat unwelcome to locals. Nowadays the caves are closed at night and

Matala has become a more ordinary little resort, very populous, and with a good but crowded beach and seafront tavernas. A rough scramble to the south leads past some decontrolled caves to a less frequented beach.

Matala is reached by turning south off the main road in Mires, after Gortyn but before Phaistos, and passing through Petrokephali and Pitsidhia, 3 miles (5km) inland. It can also be reached by striking south from Ayia Triada.

Two other spots near by on the south coast may arouse curiosity. **Lendas**, reached by a turning just before Ayii Deka, is not itself attractive—quite the reverse— but it has places to eat and sleep and there is a good beach 2 miles (3km) to the west. To the east of Lendas lie the remains of a Greek healing centre, or Asklepion, centred on what were once therapeutic springs. The Asklepion was also used during the Roman period.

Kali Limenes, reached via Mires on a moderate road, is spoiled as a resort by the presence of an oil-terminal on a small island opposite. Kali Limenes was the Biblical 'Fair Havens' where the ship carrying the prisoner Paul put in for shelter. Paul wanted to stay, but the centurion in charge of him joined forces with the ship's owner and they put out to sea— only to be engulfed by the tempestuous wind Euroclydon. They were driven on to Malta where the ship was wrecked.

Matala's visitors once took to the caves; now they prefer the beach

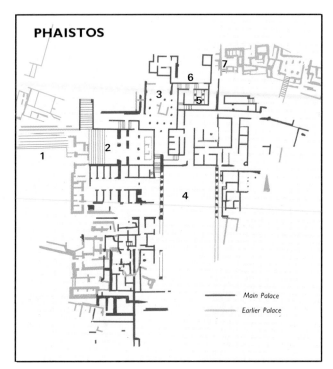

PHAISTOS

Main Palace

Earlier Palace

1 Theatre Area
2 Grand Staircase
3 Peristyle Court
4 Central Court
5 Queen's Megaron
6 King's Megaron
7 Treasury

◆◆◆
PHAISTOS (FAISTÓS)

After Knossos, Phaistos is the greatest of the Minoan palaces. It shares many key characteristics with Knossos and visitors may find it helpful to have visited Knossos first. But for important reasons, a visit to Phaistos is a completely different experience.

While Knossos is rather dowdily placed on a low hill, Phaistos is on a knoll overlooking the verdant plain of the Mesara and then out over it to mountains. Southwards lies the smallish but attractive Asterousia range, separating the Mesara from the sea. Northwards, snow-clad for half the year, is the great sweep of Mt Psiloritis, ancient Ida. (A distant blob of darkness high up on the mountain is the entrance to the sacred Kamares Cave, where worshippers left behind many examples of that fine pottery which is named after the cave.) The great beauty of the site, particularly in spring, is enough to persuade the visitor that the Minoans had a similar taste in landscape to ourselves. This feeling is reinforced by almost every other Minoan site except Knossos.

The second major difference is that Phaistos has not been reconstructed. The ruins, which are in fact extremely complex, seem at first sight both simple and, by contrast with Knossos, pure.

Phaistos was built originally round about 1900BC, but, as with Knossos and the other palaces, the first structure was destroyed in about 1700BC. A new palace was then erected on the site. Today a good deal of the Old Palace has been revealed by excavation, and old and new are puzzlingly interlaced.

The palace was excavated by an Italian team led by Federico Halbherr and Luigi Pernier. They started at the same time as Evans at Knossos, but publication of their findings came later, and therefore caused less stir.

Entry to Phaistos is across an open space usually called the Upper Court. From the southeast corner here a handsome staircase descends to the West Court, contemporary with the Old Palace. The court ended on its northern side in a wide series of steps, which remain beautiful and evocative. They must originally have been intended as seating or standing space for ritual or performance, another 'theatral area' as at Knossos.

Though not reconstructed, Phaistos gives a clear plan of the palaces

CENTRAL CRETE

Some archaeologists have speculated that bull-leaping sports, probably with some religious significance, took place here. From this position, it is easy to see the line of the front wall of the Old Palace, 23ft (7m) in front of the New. Various areas roofed in with plastic lie to south and west. These are Minoan houses outside the palace walls, currently under excavation. Now the visitor climbs yet another set of stairs, extremely handsome and slightly sunken at either side to allow rainwater to run off. These lead up to the wide west entrance of the New Palace. This entrance changes character almost at once into a warren of smaller divisions. Tucked away at a lower level are Old Palace storerooms— some with highly decorated *pithoi*.

Just to the right of the entrance in the New Palace complex were vestibules and guardrooms, a major set of storerooms and a room with lustral basin (in which ritual purifications may have taken place). A few steps further south comes a series of rooms which were clearly associated with religious worship, lying on the western side of the central court. This very fine courtyard was common to Old and New

At Phaistos the Minoan palaces looked out over the lovely Mesara plain

Palaces. In the time of the New Palace the buildings surrounding it probably stood two storeys high.

North of the courtyard are the 'royal apartments'. These apartments offer nothing as spectacular as the Grand Staircase at Knossos and were not so elaborately painted. But they too have ingenious light-wells. The materials used for the finish were very fine and the total effect was probably more pleasing if less awesome. The finest had an alabaster floor, now restored, benches round the walls and alabaster dado. The so-called King's Megaron is of characteristically Minoan arrangement, with partition of piers and door. This part of the palace had its own lustral basin and, as at Knossos, there was an indoor, water-cleansed lavatory. The so-far unreadable Phaistos Disk, with its stamped spiral of tantalising hieroglyphics, was found among Old Palace buildings just to the east. There is an acceptable café here, with a wide range of refreshments, and shelter from the hot sun.

Phaistos is 40 miles (64km) southeast of Iraklion between Mires and Tymbaki.

Accommodation

The main interest in the coastal strip right along the north of Crete lies in the hotels and beaches, which often have a fine mountain backdrop. Moving west out of Iraklion there are various hotels—and beaches—almost immediately, notably the luxury class **Creta Beach** at Amoudhari (for information about hotel gradings see **Accommodation**, page 102). This corner of coast, however, where the shoreline turns northwards, is entirely dominated by a power station. The New Road which rounds the cape leads to Ayia Pelaya, a cove with sandy bay and a promontory. It has several hotels, principally the **Capsis Beach** (tel: 081 233395). This large complex is set in gardens and has a good range of facilities, including tennis.

East from Iraklion, the New Road sets out along one of the strips of Cretan coast most thoroughly ravaged by unco-ordinated tourist development. But even amid the mess there are some good hotels.

First after the airport comes Iraklion's municipal beach (pay on entry, showers). Shortly after is Amnisos, also effectively a town beach. Then comes Hani Kokkini, which has a number of hotels, among them the A category **Arina Sand**. There is a reasonable beach here together with a mass of new building in varying states of readiness.

Gouves follows soon, offering a strange peninsula of hotels, set apart from one another on a flat projection jutting out past a fenced-in US base. The most attractive hotel here is the **Creta Sun** (tel: 0897 41241), with 345 rooms, A category.

The luxury class **Creta Maris Hotel** at the western end of Hersonisos (tel: 0897 22115) is a good substantial hotel in the block-and-bungalow vernacular and with a pretty beach, the best in the immediate area.

RETHIMNON AND ITS PROVINCE

Rethimnon and its broad strip of territory, reaching across Crete from coast to coast, commands delighted affection from its supporters. Though the 'nome', or prefecture, of Rethimnon is very mountainous, it also seems welcoming and gentle. In the spring, especially in the high valleys, it is incomparably fresh and beautiful. The surprise is to find that its seemingly relaxed and gentle people have a history of independence, rebellion and self-sacrifice stronger than almost anywhere in the island. The eastern side of the prefecture consists of the mass of Mt Psiloritis, which then drops away gently through high valleys with ancient Greek sites and Byzantine chapels. The land finally rises again towards the crags and peaks of the White Mountains in the west. The centre falls away fairly steeply to the south, pierced by valleys and at least one respectable gorge, towards a coast of bay and beach set against a mountain backdrop and interrupted by massive headlands. The northern coast, by contrast, is flat and open, mostly fringed with sandy beach, and some of it has been developed most unattractively. Rethimnon, at the centre of this coast, is a sleepy and delightful place out of season, and still seems sleepy even when busy with summer visitors. Its agreeable atmosphere makes a greater impression than its monuments, though one or two of these are striking.

RETHIMNON

Visitors entering the town from Iraklion will probably catch sight of the massive Venetian fortress, by far the most prominent feature of the town. Some little way after entry to the town, Kalergi V Street, to the right, gives access to the front, one possible point for starting a tour of Rethimnon. Equally, visitors can carry on until they reach an open space, just before a walled park, to the left, and with a large new church immediately on the right. Beyond the church, also on the right but tucked away, a Venetian gate gives access down into the old town.
On the front, you will be confronted by the town beach, a busy hoop of sand backed by grass and backed again by the promenade or *paralia* which follows along the front in both directions. It is named **Eleftheriou Venizelou**, after Crete's great modern statesman. The tourist office, NTOG, is just to your right as you reach the front. The section of the *paralia* leading left towards the fortress is closed to traffic in the evenings. Along its landward side stands a row of old houses, once very handsome. Their upper storeys have been largely remade in concrete, but their lower storeys often still survive in their original form, and incline outwards at the base as a support. These are now mostly hidden behind restaurant and cafeteria awnings.
Following onwards, keeping as close as possible to the sea, you will round the corner to reach the very pleasant horseshoe of

Crouching between sea and hills, Rethimnon has a special tranquillity

the inner harbour. Here similar old houses have survived without quite the same degree of reconstruction; these, too, are used as restaurants. Opposite are harbour sheds and, to the right, a pretty lighthouse. Beyond this a harbour mole extends out into the sea, sometimes with coastal steamers made fast alongside. A similar mole away to the right confines the eastern end of the town beach.

All this is effectively seaside Rethimnon. Just behind it is a warren of lively little streets with interesting shops. They lead the few steps inward, past a Venetian loggia now housing the Archaeological Museum (see **What to See**, below), towards **Petikhaki Square**.

One interesting route towards the square starts at the Venetian gate giving off the main road. The **Porta Guora**, as it is called, opens through a surviving fragment of Venetian town wall, leaving an isolated minaret away to the right. Ethnikis Antistaseos Street, the narrow road leading north from here to Petikhaki Square, is a real pleasure. It has everything from good bread and vegetable shops to Cretan crafts (see **Shopping**, below). Visible especially in the small streets leading off are stone-arched Venetian doorways and little boxed-in Turkish balconies made of ancient, sun-worn wood projecting at first floor level from even older houses. The road leaves, on its left, an old Venetian church converted into

Shopping is not too hectic in charming Rethimnon

a mosque by the Turks.

In a moment, you have reached Petikhaki Square, converging with the route along the front. The square is nothing special architecturally, but it has eating places and a *kafeneion* (café). Beyond it is one of the most pleasing fountains of old Crete. This, the **Arimondi Fountain**, has lost its roof but still has Corinthian capitals and a lion's head as a spout. Beyond again is the great **Venetian fortress**. Sometime during a visit to Rethimnon it is absolutely necessary to wander westwards from Petikhaki Square across the isthmus. The streets here are even more enchanting, with the same mixture of Venetian arches and Turkish balconies. There are various Turkish inscriptions and water-fountains, a little church from which plainsong chanting sometimes drifts out on the warm air, canaries hung out in cages, children scuffling about with footballs, carpenters unloading planks from small delivery vans in tiny streets—all the life of a little Greek town carrying on in parallel with tourist Crete. On the far side, the visitor will reach a larger square containing the administrative headquarters of the nome of Rethimnon.

The rest of the town, inland from the main road, is expanding fast, with modest concrete blocks and modern apartments. There is the park and another mosque, by the bus station, with the remains of a third close to Eleftheriou Venizelou. Moreover, Rethimnon has a great tradition of learning, and two of the faculties of the new university of Crete are here. So there are plenty of young people around—except, of course, during the summer vacation.

WHAT TO SEE

ARCHAEOLOGICAL MUSEUM
Palaiologo, off N end of Petikhaki Square
The museum strikes some visitors as a jumble, but in fact proceeds mainly clockwise in chronological order with exhibits from the area. Good Neolithic material, late Minoan finds from Armeni (see also Archaeological Museum, Khania), and a notable collection of Greek and Roman coins make it worth a visit.

NERANDZES MOSQUE
south of Petikhaki Square
This pleasing and delicate minaret is open to the public, and well worth seeing.

THE VENETIAN FORTRESS
This was built in 1573, and fell easily to the Turks in 1645. It has huge ramparts and battlements, and good views over the town and coast. Within the perimeter, there are a church and a former mosque, empty official buildings and a sense of abandonment and loss. The fortress is on the tip of the promontory; the main gate is at its western end.

Nightlife
Rethimnon has the ordinary run of discos plus one or two less usual venues, such as the bar-restaurant **Nikolao Gounaki** in Koronaiou Street, on the isthmus. Much hung about with Cretan 'junk', this dark dive features nightly performances on the Cretan lyre, and the singing of *mantinades*, the improvised rhyming couplets beloved of

Cretans. There are more discos (including hotel discos) along the coastal strip to the east.

Accommodation
Most of the available accommodation in the area is to the east, along the coastal strip (see page 52). Travellers passing through will find a cluster of 'B' category hotels around the two adjacent bus stations. The **Braskos** at Daskalaki 1 (tel: 0831 23721) is serviceable—and used by Greeks.

Restaurants
Rethimnon's best restaurants, or at least its fanciest, are those backing the Inner Harbour, with delicious smells of frying squid and fish, and tables grouped outdoors round the harbour. The **Taverna Vassilis** is attractive, with its masses of framed pictures, but **T'Adelphia** (The Brothers) and, really, all the others, are also worth a try. This little area gets crowded with parties visiting from elsewhere. There is a cheerful throng of less elaborate eating places round Petikhaki Square and the Arimondi Fountain, among them **Socrates 1**, **2**, and **3**! There is mass catering, with sometimes brusque service, under the awnings behind Eleftheriou Venizelou. Cafeterias on the *paralia* are enjoyed by younger people, with traditional kafeneions in Petikhaki Square and elsewhere in town.

Shopping
Rethimnon is a town of some tradition, reflected in a scatter of craft shops.
Nikos Leledaki, on the corner of

Ethnikis Antistaseos and Souliou, supplies the villages around with traditional Cretan leather boots, all hand-made and much-admired.

At Cretan Treasures, Souliou 59/Mavrokordato 8, Chris and Jacky Kalaitsidakis sell old lace, ranging from the comparatively simple to the elaborate—and proportionately pricey. You may discover fine tablecloths and place mats, curtains and many smaller lace items. The shop also commissions modern lace from villages in various parts of Crete. The Ware House Portalis, Ethnikis Antistaseos Street, and Emmanouela Markakys, by the bottom of Petikhaki Square, both sell traditional woven cloth.

THE RETHIMNON AREA

After the New Road's holiday strip which follows the shoreline to the east, a flat coastal plain gives way to a rocky and indented coastline, mountains rising above, stony valleys leading inland, the road often some way back from the coast. The road passes behind capes with hidden cliffs and beaches to rise, finally, high above Ayia Pelaya. This is the most exciting section of central Crete's north coast. There are no places of great note on the way, however—though some may like to explore the beaches of **Bali** (the best are furthest away along a side road doubling back towards the village).

There are two ways of travelling inland to Iraklion, cutting off the corner of coast round which the New Road runs; both ways, however, are much slower. The first possibility is to use the Iraklion Old Road running through the foothills via Perama. This winds on through the villages of Mourtzana, Drosia, Damasta and Marathos, passes by the cone of Mt Stroumboulas and so to Iraklion.

When passing through Perama, there is a possible turning 2½ miles (4km) to the left to the **Melidhoni Cave**, which has been associated with the mythical giant Talos. He is said to have marched round the island keeping strangers off. During the insurrection against the Turks in the 1820s it became a mass grave for nearly 300 local people. After they had taken refuge here, their Turkish assailants blocked the mouth of the cave and then lit fires, asphyxiating those within.

The second route to Iraklion also starts off through Perama but then, shortly after Mourtzana, angles obliquely to the southeast, sweeping round in a shallow semi-circle to rejoin the Old Road again some 4 miles (7km) from Iraklion. This road winds up the northern flank of Psiloritis, ascending through Garazo and Axos to Anoyia before it drops down again. The place most people want to visit is Anoyia—though the whole road is very scenic.

The coast road west traverses the plain, behind a shoreline of sandy beach. Until the vicinity of Yeoryioupolis and first views of the White Mountains it is actually quite a boring road. Excursions inland, however, will reward with glimpses of an older Crete. The road south climbs up towards Armeni, where late Minoan burials have been

excavated in recent years.
Seven miles (11km) later comes
the first opportunity to turn right
for Plakias on a route which
leads down through the Farangi
Kotsifou, the Kotsifou Gorge. A
mile (2km) later another possible
descent leaves the main road,
starting off through Koxare, half a
mile (1km) off the main road.
This winds its way down through
the increasingly spectacular
Koutaliotiko Gorge. Do not be
too alarmed even if you are
arriving for the first time at
night—others have got down
safely before you.

*The handsome monastery of Arkadi,
once a guerilla stronghold, is a
byword for heroism*

THE AMARI VALLEY

The south coast can be reached
from Rethimnon via the high
Amari Valley, lying close in
under Psiloritis to the west. Take
the road inland from Perivolia,
just at the eastern edge of
Rethimnon, then up through
Prasies and Filakio to Thronos at
the head of the valley. The road
divides soon afterwards, the
eastern side hugging the valley
closely, the road to the west
swinging away from it in places.
This is some of the loveliest
landscape in Crete; the area is
rich in antiquities and Byzantine
chapels. Not all are easily
accessible and visitors intending
to explore more fully may wish to
consult a specialist guide book
(see **Directory** entry, **Guide
Books**). At the southern end of
the Amari Valley it is possible to
turn east for Zaros, Ayia Varvara
and Iraklion or to continue south
for Ayia Galini and the Mesara.

WHAT TO SEE IN THE RETHIMNON AREA

◆ ANOYIA

Anoyia is a mountain village with
a bitter modern history. When
General Kreipe, the German
commander in Crete, was
abducted by the resistance and
taken off the island during World
War II, Anoyia was one of the
villages which sheltered his
captors—and, indeed, helped to
hide General Kreipe. With the
exception of the church, the
village was destroyed in
reprisal. Since the war, it has
resurrected itself through
weaving and handicrafts and,
almost as soon as tourism began,
established itself as *the* village
for hosting parties for 'Cretan
evenings'. If it now seems more
commercialised than other
places, this is the reason. And if
some of the textiles insistently
exhibited are less than
wonderful, that is because
tourists will buy them. All this

being said, the village has a fine
position, is alive and active and
can be a very good place to stop,
especially in winter.

It is also the starting point for
excursions to the **Idaean Cave**,
very high up on Psiloritis. This
may or may not have been the
cave where Zeus was born
(some plump for the Diktean
Cave above the Lasithi plateau)
but it became a major place of
pilgrimage for the classical
Greek world. Pythagoras and
the Cretan philosopher
Epimonides paid it a joint visit.
Today, the cave is fenced off to
protect excavations in progress.
For details of the trail, ask locally
or consult a guide book with
routes for walkers.

◆◆◆
THE MONASTERY OF ARKADI
*11 miles (18km) southeast of
Rethimnon*
During the 19th century this
monastery in the hills was at the
centre of the Cretan
independence movement,
supporting resistance to the
Turks. When Turkish assailants
were on the point of breaching
the walls during the rising of
1866, the defenders responded,
so it is claimed, by putting a
torch to their powder magazine.
However it happened, there was
certainly a mighty blast. Much of
the building still stands—the
powder magazine is roofless—
but the force of the explosion
killed hundreds of attackers and
a great number of the men,
women and children gathered
within the monastery. The name
of Arkadi was blazoned across
the world, a code-word for
heroism.

The monastery gate has been
rebuilt. The church, somewhat
pitted in places from the
explosion, dates from 1587 and
has one of the most decorative,
and handsome, of all façades in
Crete. The monastery has a
small museum. A monument
near by contains the skulls of
some of those who died that day
in November, 1866.

◆◆
AYIA GALINI
Ayia Galini is the most popular
and populous resort of the
central part of the south coast of
Crete. It occupies a narrow
cranny of valley ending in a
quarter circle of harbour with
fishing boats and tourist boats,
and a general sense of activity.
The back end of the valley,
where the road enters, has been
the scene of recent and prolific

endeavours in concrete. You reach the sea by passing along busy little streets full of small restaurants and tourist shops. The front has a finished and settled air, with terraced 'rent rooms' establishments and tiny hotels climbing up a little rock face to the east. Every building on the front is a restaurant or café or tourist shop, or is hung with signs pointing on to yet another. Tamarisk, hibiscus and bougainvillea are all on show. It seems to be the very sense of confinement that the crowds enjoy—though in summer it is no place for claustrophobics. There is no listed hotel above 'C' grade, a fact which gives some indication of the cheap and cheerful atmosphere.

Ayia Galini is on the south coast, reached from Rethimnon on the road which passes through Spili.

Ayia Galini, once a small fishing port is now the south coast's most popular resort, attracting holidaymakers in droves.

◆◆
PLAKIAS

High and fissured mountains, grey in colour, rise behind this village. The coastal hills tip forward to form a semi-circular bay with Plakias and its tiny harbour lying a little towards the west. The eastern end of the bay is closed off by a high crag. This is the prettiest setting of any coastal village in Crete, though it is not necessarily the friendliest place. One feels that development is arriving rather suddenly, perhaps disconcertingly. There is now a group of package hotels on the front here with one or two outlying establishments to the east. Building is progressing apace along the one little road that runs back from the front. The stony beach stretching eastwards can be windy, and bathers often build themselves makeshift walls for shelter. There are discos and places to eat and have a coffee, and nothing very much more—but more will undoubtedly arrive. There are other striking villages behind Plakias on the mountainside.

Plakias is on a turning to the right on the southward road from Rethimnon, 7 miles (11km) from Armeni.

MONASTERY OF PREVELI
From Plakias it is a short drive east, well in behind the coast, towards the monastery of Preveli. The road passes through a ravishing little valley, tender against its background of mountain. The turn down to Preveli passes a handsome 19th-century bridge, and then the very venerable ruins of the 16th-century monastic foundation out of which the present (17th-century) Preveli has grown. The road reaches the coast up above the beach from which Allied escapees from the Battle of Crete were taken off the island by submarine. A memorial tablet tells of 'the ferocious German reprisals' suffered by monks and villagers who 'fed, protected and helped' the hundreds of Allied troops. It then hooks round to reach the monastery, with only the barest minimum of monks remaining.

This important monastery reported directly to the Patriarch in Constantinople and became extremely wealthy—a fact hard to believe today, given its isolated position. Like Arkadi, it was a source of continuous resistance to Turkish occupation and, like Arkadi, it participated in the 1866 rising. The tradition of independence was still alive at the time of World War II, when Preveli was used as a rallying point for Allied soldiers left behind after the Battle of Crete. A broad terrace with a splendid shade tree looks down over a slope with olives, cypresses and perhaps a grazing flock of sheep. The monastery church is 19th century. Rules of dress are strictly applied.

Accommodation
The New Road towards Iraklion follows the shoreline east, leaving just enough room between itself and the sea for both the Old Road and a ribbon of tourist development, most dense from Platanias on. This is a real mess, distressingly ugly, full of ill-assorted buildings, but lively even so. In the standard Cretan manner, several perfectly pleasant hotels and one particularly good one are located amid the mess. The good hotel is the **Rithymna Beach Hotel** (tel: 0831 71002). With 600 rooms, this is a community in itself. Despite a somewhat unfortunate khaki colour—quite common in contemporary Crete—it has all kinds of facilities, including a conference room and supervised camping on the beach for children whose parents are staying in the hotel. The Rithymna Beach is very popular with families.

KHANIA AND THE WEST

Western Crete has more capacity to astound than other parts of the island. Though not as high as Psiloritis in the centre, the White Mountains are far more awesome; the coast of the extreme west, despite magnificent beaches, is wild and little visited; the high rock wall of the southwest stands up out of the Libyan sea with impressive austerity. Most memorable of all, perhaps, the southern side of the White Mountains is cleft by the great Gorge of Samaria. Though heavily walked, the gorge remains quite beautiful. Add to this Khania, reckoned by many to be the most vibrant and delightful of Crete's large towns; and add a people who are often dramatic, but open and friendly at the same time, and Western Crete offers a heady mix. The Minoans were here in force, as we shall see, but their main places of habitation are still a mystery. Early and Classical Greek remains are remote and only enthusiasts will search them out—though some of the ruins are both impressive and wonderfully sited. There are Venetian monuments, a mass of Byzantine fresco painting, and Turkish minarets; and moving World War II cemeteries which many may wish to visit. But on the whole the visitor will probably spend more time with beach and landscape than on the cultural trail.

Most of the places to stay are in a coastal strip to the west of Khania, on the whole cheerful and enjoyed, but once again bearing signs of hasty and ill-co-ordinated assembly. From here, a proper visit to Khania is a must on any list. In addition, there are a variety of excursions to be made into the countryside and mountains, some in the course of a day, others taking longer.

Ancient Aptera near Souda Bay was a powerful Greco-Roman city-state going back to the 7th century BC

KHANIA

Of Crete's major towns, it is Khania which has won the plaudits over the last ten or 20 years. This popularity is due not so much to Khania's monuments as to its bracing position under the White Mountains, the thoroughly Cretan vigour of its inhabitants and the variety of its trades, from the manufacture of Cretan knee-boots to the carving of ornate and fairly dreadful furniture.

Much of modern Khania was destroyed by a firestorm during the Battle of Crete in 1941 and has since been rebuilt and enlarged. But in the old quarter round the harbour, narrow, handsome little streets survive, with high houses on either side

*Khania's picturesque harbour is a
pleasant place to wander or sit*

For at least two decades,
Khania's old harbour has been
recognised as the most attractive
of all harboursides in Crete and
the biggest single reason for the
popularity of the city. At present,
however, mass tourism
combines with the continuing
presence of Greek and
American military bases on the
Akrotiri peninsula to make things
seem rather seedy here,
particularly at night. Yet one
would certainly wish to eat here
at least once in a stay of any
length, and one or two of the
harbour-front lodging houses are
most appealing (see
Accommodation, below).
Plateia 1866, the square at the
top of Halidon Street, is one of
the focal points of town, where
the main road from Iraklion and
Rethimnon comes closest to the
harbour. With its trees and
shade and glimpses of the
mountains, this square has a
reasonable claim to being the
centre of the city. It is the main
stop for most city buses. The bus
station proper is by its top end
and the market, one of Khania's
principal buildings, is just a little
way back to the east.
Halidon Street, not especially
attractive in itself, is the main
venue for fast food, quick-buy
jewellery and tourist shops.
Streets leading off it are the best
place for leather (see **Shopping**,
below). On the right of the street,
towards the harbour, there is a
paved open space with Khania's
19th-century **cathedral** at the
back of it; an unexciting edifice.
Here, in 1770, the Cretan hero

in states of interesting
dilapidation. Some of them are
built into Venetian defensive
walls. There is also an area of
dignified neo-classical
splendour from the period at the
turn of the century when Crete
was an international protectorate
with its capital here at Khania.
The city remained the island's
capital till 1971.

Ioannis Daskaloyiannis was flayed alive after surrendering himself to the Turks at the castle of Frangokastello in the south. Almost at once, to the left on Halidon, comes the door to the old church which houses Khania's **Archaeological Museum**.

Within just a few paces, the visitor will now reach a little open space known generally as **Habour Square** (technically the Plateia Sindrivani). Looking straight out across the water from the point of arrival on the front, there is a good view of one of the trademarks of Khania, the elegant **lighthouse** built by the Venetians and restored by the Egyptians during a brief period of control in the 1830s. Immediately to the right is a steep-sided hill, appropriately named **Kastelli**, the site first

fortified by the Venetians and from which all later Khania has sprung. Parts of it are shored up still above the harbour by very old Venetian walls. On the left, the harbour front curves round in a half-circle of beautiful old buildings, the Akti Koundourioti. Between the water and the raised bulk of Kastelli, there are two interesting free-standing buildings. The first is the Hotel Plaza, with a Venetian fountain tucked in just underneath its entrance. The second, the purpose-built but rather drab Mosque of the Janissaries, now houses the Tourist Office on one side and a restaurant/café on the other. Behind and carrying on round the corner to the right, along a section of the front called

The Mosque of the Janissaries and Plaza hotel flank Khania harbour

Akti Tombazi, are more buildings of considerable age, restaurants and discos and eventually the shell of a large Venetian building now under reconstruction. Next comes a series of ruinous Venetian arsenali or warehouses. This last section of the front, lying along an inner harbour busy with fishing boats and yachts, is called Akti Enoscos.

Past the point where Halidon meets the outer harbour is the semi-circle of **Akti Koundouriotou**. Every one of the fine old houses here appears to have a restaurant, bar or café at its base, the awnings hiding much of the handsome architectural detail—steps, for example, mounting on a half arch up to a first-floor door. On the far corner of the hoop of harbour front, there is a **Naval Museum** (see below). Passing through the entrance here, you can reach the inner part of the **Firkas**, the Venetian fortification on the tip of this side of the bay. Here, in 1913, the Greek national flag was hoisted officially for the first time in Crete. The Akti Koundouriotou is the great tourist trap of Khania but one in which the visitor will want at some point to be caught. It is this area and the network of streets behind which sometimes seem a little threatening at night.

Above and behind this part, however, there is a small area of great beauty and considerable antiquity. **Theotokopoulou Street** (named for El Greco) is its principal thoroughfare, running back from the sea along the top of the promontory with fine old wrought-iron balconies and

narrow alleyways leading off. One of the features of this part of town is the somewhat buried Venetian masonry of the **Renieri Gate**.

First-time visitors to Khania will probably want to begin by getting the feel of the harbour area and then radiate outwards. In this progression, Kastelli is the next place to visit—because it is near, because it is beautiful in its dilapidated way and because of the Minoan connection.

Khania was known to the ancient Greeks by the name of Kydonia, and archaeologists increasingly suspect that Kydonia may have become the principal settlement of Crete after the final destruction of Knossos. There is a strong presumption that there was a major Minoan palace here, perhaps on the Kastelli hill. No trace of it has yet been found, but a recent dig has been turning up high quality late Minoan finds. The site itself is not a palace but the goods are of palatial type; many are now in the museum. Perhaps the visitor is at this point standing very close to buried treasure of the most spectacular kind.

Kydonia was a lively city-state during the classical Greek centuries, prospered under the Romans and continued to do well in the first Byzantine period. It later experienced a substantial period as the Venetian capital of Crete. Kastelli having been the site of the first fortifications, it is no surprise that Venetian memorials can be found on top among the decaying houses, lively now with younger visitors and pensions. Round the back of Kastelli, in Sifaka and Karaoli

The pace of a horse-drawn carriage is ideal for Khania's streets

Streets, there are interesting stretches where old walls and later houses are inextricably interlaced.

Beyond Kastelli one enters a part of town called Spiantza, with narrow streets, architectural oddities and churches which did duty as mosques during Turkish rule (in Khania, from 1645 to 1898).

Carrying on behind the coast one finally reaches **Halepa**— which is further than it seems and may justify the use of a car or a taxi. From 1898, during the period between the end of Turkish dominance and final union with Greece, Crete was first ruled by the Greek crown prince, under the eye of the Great Powers. The prince and his diplomats had their residences in Halepa and a little of this faded dignity endures.

To the west from Halepa is Khania's main market, a large cruciform building, drawing together a fine selection of produce, much from western Crete. The market is positively swollen with fish and vegetables, tobaccos and teas, strings of sausages and carcasses of goats and any other foodstuff you can buy in Crete. Its comparative order and sense of loftiness provide a strong contrast with the market of Iraklion and those who wish to linger may like to try one of the small restaurants among the stalls.

Across the road from the market, two rather more formal, European-type streets lead away southeast. These are Dimokratias and Tzanakakis, with Khania's Public Gardens opening out between them some four blocks down from the market. Both have modern shops, airline offices, etc, and the latter leads on to the Historical Museum. To either side, east and west and surprisingly extensive, the modern city of Khania stretches out.

WHAT TO SEE

ARCHAEOLOGICAL MUSEUM
Halidon Street
This is in an old church, much beset by time but with an agreeable garden and appealing fountain. Exhibits, running roughly clockwise through time, feature most prominently a Minoan progression from western Crete, including important finds from Kastelli. In the centre are the fine tombs found in Armeni, near Rethimnon.

HISTORICAL MUSEUM AND ARCHIVES
20 Sphakianakis Street, off end of Tzanakakis
Memorials of the statesman Venizelos, intimately associated with Khania, and of the struggle for independence which he brought at last to a successful conclusion.

NAVAL MUSEUM
Akti Koundouriotou
Models, photographs and an interesting display of naval history.

Accommodation
Most visitors stay on the holiday strip to the west of the city. In town, there is the 'A' class **Kydon** (tel: 0821 26190), just near the market, and several hotels around the bus station—the friendly **Samarias**, 'B' class (tel: 0821 51551); the **Omalos**, next door, 'C' class (tel: 0821 57171) and the **Canea**, just round the corner on 1866 Square (tel: 0821 24673). On the front, if you can bear the throb of music, is the 30-bed **Amphora** (tel: 0821 4200), the prettiest building on the harbour, incorporating Venetian and Turkish elements and decorated with elegant simplicity. Just round the corner from the Firkas and seemingly an integral if ugly part of the city's defences, is the **Hotel Xenia** (tel: 0821 24562).

Nightlife
The most favoured discos are **Ariadni**, to the right along the front, and the **Agora**, tucked into a corner of the market (around the east end of the building and up a flight of stairs). The **Fagotto** on Agelou Street features jazz bands and jazz piano. Bouzouki and performances by leading Greek performers—very loud—can be enjoyed out of town at **Khania by Night** (it may be easiest to go by taxi). There are more discos along the coastal strip to the west.

Restaurants
Locals say the best fish restaurant in town is the unpretentious **Dino's** behind Akti Enoseos, the inner harbour.

Dull brown decor but marvellous squid, cuttlefish, prawns, octopus, etc, as well as straightforward fish. Other good fish restaurants may be found near by and on the front in the New Town, half a mile (1km) or so out west beyond the Naval Museum. Inevitably one will also eat in the outer harbour—Greek style starters, fish and traditional Greek dishes. **The Meltemi**, by the Naval Museum, is a reasonable place to have a drink on the harbour front, though there are many other bars and cafés here and elsewhere in town. The little road running inland just beyond the Arsenals is alive with young Greeks during university term.

Shopping

Khania is one of the best places on the island for hand-made Cretan goods; and there is a concentration of craft shops in Agelou, Theotokopoulou and Zambeliu Streets, behind the outer harbour.

For Cretan weaving, try Kosta at 5 Agelou Street. He claims his collection of fabrics is between 50 and 130 years old and they are priced accordingly. The colours are rich and lovely, with varying degrees of elaboration in the weaving. Many of these items were made originally for dowries.

At Roka, 61 Zambeliu, in sharp contrast, the owner's elderly mother sits at a loom in the shop-

Khania is a good place to look for exciting hand-made Cretan products

front weaving traditional designs and producing rugs and bags. The interior is especially attractive.

At 12 Zambeliu a tiny jewellery shop sells gold and silver jewellery in traditional and modern styles, with a little workshop to the rear. 81 Zambeliu shows hand-made Cretan ceramics, including the work of two local potters. Soft blues are a speciality. On the top of the hill, at 19 Theotokopoulou, Aura, a Danish designer's shop, offers well-made jewellery in an elegant display.

Back in Halidon Street, tourist knick-knacks and cheaper jewellery are on sale. Skridlof leading off to the right, as one descends, is the best place for leather goods. These can be very varied in quality. Smell the leather before you buy; if it smells rough here, it will smell worse at home. Belts, bags and lace can all be found in this area.

WHAT TO SEE IN WESTERN CRETE

AKROTIRI

The name Akrotiri means peninsula. The peninsula in question is the large, ear-shaped tract of land that juts up immediately northeast of Khania. The city's airport is roughly at its centre. Akrotiri is also a hot spot for military activity—whence the great number of military personnel taking their ease along with the tourists in Khania's bars and restaurants. The bases mean blank walls down on the flat and radar installations on mountain tops. In addition, Souda Bay, bounded on the north by

Akrotiri (see below), is the site of a major naval base regarded with great sensitivity by Greek security. The no-camera signs mean just that.

Despite all this, Akrotiri offers some notable modern history, good scenery, fine beaches and several particularly interesting monasteries.

The modern history is soon encountered. Where the Khania-Akrotiri road ends its climb up to the high neck of the peninsula, a turning left leads on to the hill of **Profitis Ilias** (the Prophet Elijah), with magnificent views back over Khania. In 1897, Cretan rebels raised the Greek flag on these heights and kept it flying despite bombardment by an international peace-keeping fleet. Later, Eleftherios Venizelos, statesman and the architect of the island's unity with Greece, was buried here. The plainness of his grave (he is buried with his son Sophocles) makes an emphatic memorial. From here, the turning north leads on past Kalathas (two small beaches) to **Stavros**, a notable circular bay and beach. The far side is bounded by a steep fall of mountain—familiar to many from the final scenes of the film version of *Zorba the Greek*.

To visit Akrotiri's monasteries, take the right turn at Kounoupidiana, a mile (2km) along the main road past the Venizelos grave, then left as sign-posted 4 miles (6km) later (leaving the airport to southeast). The first monastery is **Ayia Triada**. This very handsome Venetian structure, founded by a Venetian convert to Orthodoxy and pierced by one of the most grandiose entrances on Crete, has sonorous echoes despite its present decay. The **Monastery of Gouverneto** is a few miles further along a less impressive, though attractive, road. A few minutes further along again, now on foot, comes the **cave of St John the Hermit**, an important local saint, and finally, after about 45 minutes' walk in all, the long-abandoned **Monastery of Katholiko**, spectacularly positioned by a stone bridge crossing the bottom of a cleft.

A sun-drenched corner in one of the monasteries of the Akrotiri peninsula

GAVDHOS ISLAND
*31 miles (50km) south of
Paleohora*
Gavdhos is the biblical Clauda
past which St Paul's vessel was
driven on its way to shipwreck in
Malta nearly 2,000 years ago. It is
the largest and most southerly of
Crete's island dependencies.
Gavdhos is interesting mainly
because it is there; the people,
though friendly, are few and not
having an easy time, and the
landscape is mild and unexciting
compared to Crete. Even
knowing this, one somehow has
a strong urge to see it; and
goodly numbers gratify that
urge. The boat from Paleohora
lands at Karabe. Then comes an
hour's gradual climb on foot to
Kastri, the village which serves
as the island's capital. Only a
handful of families remain here.
For visitors prepared to walk the
several miles north or south,
there is good swimming at the
island's extremities. Water,
however, is in short supply and
food is limited.

MALEME
AND THE NORTHWEST
west of Khania
Maleme is reached on the main
road west from Khania, some
miles after Germany's memorial
to its paratroopers—a diving
eagle—and a strip of ragged
tourist development.
Maleme has long had a little
airstrip. In order to capture
Crete in May 1941, General Karl
Student, the German
commander, needed to control,
at a bare minimum, one of the
island's north coast airstrips (the

others were at Rethimnon and
Iraklion). At Maleme paratroops
and gliders landed successfully,
and during that night, the Allies
retreated from the hill above the
airstrip—'Hill 107'. General
Student opened up this
weakness in the Allied wall,
pouring men and munitions into
Crete through the tiny airstrip of
Maleme.
Shortly before Maleme airstrip, a
turning up to the left leads on to
the former Hill 107, now the site
of the German War Cemetery.
Just off the road leading up to the
war cemetery, there is an
elaborate Minoan tomb.
Shortly, a road strikes off southwest to Paleohora—the route
which most visitors take. But
Crete's far west, even if
relatively little visited, is a
spectacular part of the island.
Initially, the landscape is
dominated by the two capes that
stick up from the island's head
like insect antennae. The first is
Rodopou. At its base on the
nearer or eastern side is the
small town of **Kolimbari**, looking
back towards Khania. There is
an ancient monastery here with
outstanding icons and a modern
seminary for Orthodox priests.
Boats can be hired for trips north
to **Diktynna**, site of an important
Greco-Roman temple, now
thoroughly ruined.
Once across the high ground at
the base of Rodopou, a wide
view opens out across the Gulf of
Kissamou to right, over the plain
backing the town of Kastelli, and
on beyond the gulf to the even
wilder Gramvousa peninsula.
Kastelli, known as Kastelli
Kissamou, has an unemphatic
ease, with a little scrap of square

in the middle where passers-by can get a meal, more tavernas down on the front and the start of tourist development. There is a twice-weekly ferry to the island of Kythera and on to the Peloponnese. The plain behind Kastelli is rich in oranges and olives, and on a steep crag 4 miles (6km) to the south lie the ruins of the ancient city of Polyrhinnia.

Beyond again, towards the western coast and then a short way north, the ruins of an ancient port named **Phalasarna** can be found high and dry above the sea. The sands here are magnificent—but beware of oil on the beach. Southwards, a wonderfully rustic though sometimes alarming road leads right down the whole of the far western coast (a distance of some 15 miles, 24km) via the nunnery of **Khrysoskalitissa** to a point where it is possible to wade across the shallows to the shadeless but idyllic island of **Elafonisi**. In good weather, Elafonisi can also be reached by boat from Paleohora.

The whole of this western coast together with the roads and villages inland, must rank high among the most beautiful areas of Crete.

◆◆
PALEOHORA (PALAIOKHÓRA), AND THE ROAD FROM KHANIA

The road west out of Khania turns south at Tavronitis to start its ascent via the large village of Voukoulies, a fruit and vegetable growing area, with an active Saturday market. Climbing more steeply, with some fine views

down over the Maleme coast and the Rodopou peninsula, the road eventually breasts a ridge and drops down into a wide and pleasingly contoured plain. All around there are churches with Byzantine frescoes, some well-preserved, many ruinous, sometimes disfigured with a chalky film of white. The village of Anisaraki, on the Temenia road out of Kandanos, has no fewer than four Byzantine chapels; there are two at Kakodiki just on past Kandanos; and many, many more in the general vicinity.

Shortly the road begins its descent to Paleohora. The dominant feature is a ruined Venetian castle on a rocky

outcrop, with the town tucked in behind across the isthmus.

As the main road comes into town it turns into a pretty little street, increasingly crammed with tourist shops and restaurants. These spill out to fill the whole street in the evening and traffic is diverted along the front, to the left. Here there is a pebble beach and sea-front restaurants, and a small harbour for local boats, including the south coast ferry.

On the west of the isthmus, a long sandy beach backed by tamarisk trees provides some of the best bathing on Crete. It can be windy, though, and this makes it a leading spot for practised wind-surfers.

The south-coast ferry from Paleohora to Ayia Roumeli puts in at Souyia as a first stop. This little port and hamlet with a long beach has become something of a magnet for young travellers and will presumably evolve into a resort. It can also be reached overland from Khania and by a roundabout road from Paleohora via Kandanos. From Souyia, it is possible to walk or take a village boat back just a little west to Lissos, an ancient Dorian settlement which survived into Greco-Roman times as a healing centre.

The beach at Ayia Roumeli, a haven of rest for weary walkers arriving from the Samaria Gorge

◆◆◆

SAMARIA GORGE

This is an excursion that many people will want to make, and very properly, since the gorge is extremely beautiful. Visitors should be aware, however, that in high season so many others make the trek that it is scarcely possible to pause and look upwards at the splendours one has come to see.

The descent of the gorge is a long 10 miles (16km), hard on the legs and knees and demanding good footwear. The gorge is open only from May to October because of the fierce flash-flooding that can occur, sometimes with fatal consequences. So, though Samaria is an extremely popular hike, it is also an undertaking.

Khania is the nearest starting point, but the excursion can be made by coach from many other tourist centres. The most enjoyable tours are those which start from the nearer resorts, reach the gorge early and allow walkers to make the descent before it gets too hot. The further away you start, the hotter and wearier you will be by the end. Samaria-bound buses first make their way up and up to the pancake-flat, mountain-ringed plain of Omalos, a word meaning belly-button. This plain, regarded by at least some of the ancient Greeks as the navel of the world, was the scene of a famous meeting of rebel leaders during the Cretan revolt of 1866. It is celebrated in a folksong which was often performed as a gesture of defiance in nightclubs and other places of entertainment under the dictatorship of the Greek Colonels during the 1970s.

The buses decant their passengers near a useful drinks stall. Those doing the walk then begin an immediate descent, with a thrilling rock face opposite, down a well-built zig-zag path called the Xyloskalo, or Wooden Stairs. The path drops through perhaps 1,000ft (300m) in half a mile (1km), amid the fresh smell of cypresses, glimpses of the rock face opposite and with a pocket of blue sky above. It is advisable to take refreshments, but there are several springs, and some may want to carry bottles and fill them at the springs. The route levels out when it joins the stream bed at the bottom of the valley. But the going gets rough underfoot, with only loose rocks to walk on now for most of the remainder of the journey. If you can manage to look up, you will see trees clinging crazily to the cliffs above, birds wheeling and, always, a sense of grandeur and loftiness.

Walkers soon come across a little church, and then the abandoned village of **Samaria**, on the far side of the stream rather less than halfway through the walk. There is a public toilet and plenty of people picnic on the grass round about. Then comes another little church, and, after a long interval, the walker arrives at the Iron Gates, or **Sideresportes**. This is the point where the high rock walls of the gorge narrow to about 15ft (5m), with the stream, sometimes a flood, tumbling between them. It is the high point of the gorge

experience.

After this, a fairly long stretch leads on to **Old Ayia Roumeli**, a semi-abandoned village with several pretty peasant courtyards and two small shops selling drinks and postcards. This is followed by a hot and dull final stretch across a diffuse stony terrain to the modern settlement of **Ayia Roumeli**. Considering that it has no road, this little place has become astonishingly active, with masses of building and cement and a

Only fit walkers should attempt a hike through the Samaria Gorge

harbour in process of construction at the west end of the shingle beach. The beach itself shelves sharply so that within a step or two the deliciously cool water is bearing the weight of the weary walker. There are meals and drinks to be had here in plenty. At the appointed hour, with any luck, the boat service will ferry you on to Hora Sfakion. This is a fine boat-ride under an imposing coast, with a possible stop in **Loutro**, a tiny semi-circle of village backing an almost perfectly round bay. Loutro is accessible only by boat or on foot and remains one of the most charming places on Crete.

It is also possible to make the Samaria walk on trips starting in Paleohora to the west. There is a boat service back to Paleohora, via Souyia. The journey west is tremendous, the ferry feeling perilously small under great falls of cliff. What appears to be a waterline some way up on the cliff face is precisely that; the southwest coast of Crete has risen by approximately 26ft (8m) since classical antiquity.

Loutro, accessible only from the cliffs or the sea, is a gem

SFAKIA

southeast of Khania on the south coast of the island

The high, bare landscapes of Sfakia are somewhat dispirited today and badly depopulated but, Minoan sites aside, this is the most celebrated region in the island. With its capital at Hora Sfakion and its territory running from the island's backbone down to the south coast, Sfakia is famous for a long list of attributes. First comes its past ferocity, expressed as heroism or brigandage depending on circumstances, but traditionally combined with intense loyalty to its own people. Then there was its sense of independence, extreme even for Crete. Sfakia was also known for huge and bombastic

boastfulness; and for the deep, rich seams of folklore which have helped give it so strong a sense of itself.

It probably derived much of its character from centuries of isolation behind its mountain barrier. Writers from the 17th century onwards describe the Sfakiots in the most vivid terms. All males bore arms—this was true up to World War II and beyond. They practised the vendetta and bride-stealing, they believed in vampires, and men and women alike were tremendous dancers. The Sfakiots were the originators of many serious revolts against the Turks—disregarding the retribution wreaked on the lowlanders—and they themselves frequently raided the lowlands. During World War II, the Sfakiots behaved with the courage and dignity that might have been expected from the more serious side of their legend, first sheltering the Allied troops left behind after the Battle of Crete and then taking an important role in the resistance. The road south from Vryses, a pleasant village south of the New Road, about 20 miles (30km) southeast of Khania, soon begins to climb towards Sfakia. The church of the Panayia in **Alikambos**, a left turn 3 miles (5km) from Vryses, has fine 14th-century frescoes by Ioannis Pagomenos. He was one of only a few painters to sign his work, which is surprisingly prolific in western Crete.

Back on the main road, the traveller is following the route taken by the Allied Army in May 1941, on their desperate retreat.

Having climbed to a considerable altitude, the road crosses the plain of Askifou, passing the village of Amoudhari and, further on, Imbros. From here, it is possible to walk down towards the coast inside the fine Imbros ravine. After Imbros, the road itself soon comes out on to open slopes, with wide views beneath and a sense of exposure, as you track your way down through hairpin bends. At the bottom, turn right for Hora Sfakion, and left for Frangokastello.

Hora Sfakion (Khóra Sfakión) (often simply called Sfakia) will not detain the visitor for long. Once Sfakia had its own fleet and the town was famous for the number of its churches. Now it is a nonentity of a place, with tavernas and rooms to rent and a waterfront plaque to commemorate the evacuation of troops by the British navy in May 1941.

From Hora Sfakion, boats leave for the bottom of the **Samaria Gorge**, and, more importantly, the boats bring back to Sfakia the many walkers who have already descended through the gorge with organised tours. These tours start in the plain of Omalos in the centre of the massif.

A road uphill to the west leads to the substantial Sfakiot village of **Anopolis** on a high plain under the White Mountains. Anopolis was the home of Ioannis Daskaloyiannis, the greatest Sfakiot hero of all—memory of him lives on partly because his deeds are the subject of a Cretan verse epic. Egged on by agents of Catherine the Great of

Russia, Daskaloyiannis raised the flag against Turkey in 1770. He eventually surrendered after the capture of his brother and was ultimately tortured to death in the cathedral square in Khania. Turkish reprisals broke the power of Sfakia, which has never since recovered. Despite depopulation, Anopolis retains a settled feeling.

Returning eastwards along the coast and passing the point where the main road comes in from Vryses, the first major event is the Venetian castle of **Frangokastello**. This splendid honey-coloured castle, visible on the right and reached most easily by the second of the turnings which lead down to it, is nothing more than a shell.

In 1828, during the War of Independence, the mainland Greek leader Hadzi Mikali Daliani took up position here and rashly met the Turks in open battle. He and his troops were annihilated, but there is a local legend that their ghosts can still be seen in springtime on the anniversary of the battle. They are called the Dhrosoulites, or Dew Shadows.

◆
SOUDA (SOÚDHA)
east of Khania by the Old Road
This long deep-water inlet, with a fortified island at its mouth and Akrotiri to the north, has for many centuries been the main anchorage and the centre of naval power on Crete, just as it is today. The large and poignant Allied War Cemetery is at the base of the bay, and then comes Souda itself, a drably functional little place with adequate

facilities for passengers arriving and departing on the Piraeus ferries.

New Road and Old Road merge at this point, and after the merging of routes, the road sweeps along the south coast of Souda Bay. There is a large-scale Venetian fortification at Kalami, and a spectacular view of Souda Bay for those coming in the opposite direction. Mid-way across the water, the fortifications of Souda Island look misleadingly like something out of toytown. The island in fact held out against the Turks for nearly 50 years after the fall of Iraklion.

Accommodation
Most accommodation in western Crete is in Khania or along the coastal strip to its west. Among several small hotels in the little town of Kastelli Kissamou (see above), the **Elena Beach** (tel: 0822 23300), to the west, is moderately promising.

The **Chandris Crete** (tel: 0821 62221) is a large hotel set just behind the beach in Maleme. There are several modest but acceptable hotels in Paleohora.

Ayios Nikolaos

AYIOS NIKOLAOS AND EASTERN CRETE

In Ayios Nikolaos, eastern Crete possesses the island's best known resort. Though this is a pretty place, deserving its mild celebrity status, there is more to be found in eastern Crete. Compared to the Khania region, the east end of the island is almost gentle in its scenery; but it is still more rugged than, say, Corfu or Rhodes, and its villages often reflect an old and thoroughly Cretan lifestyle.

The entry to eastern Crete—the prefecture of Lasithi—leaves the Dikte mountain range to the right. Then comes the outstanding Gulf of Mirabello, with Ayios Nikolaos on its nearer side along with much smaller but

Old chapel against the backcloth of historic Souda Bay, a restful spot away from the tourist trail

more up-market Elounda. The famous island of Spinalonga is just off Elounda, while 6 miles (10km) south of Ayios Nikolaos the hill village of Kritsa offers the best of Cretan weaving, a stunning Byzantine church and a side-trip to a set of ruggedly dramatic Dorian remains.

Past Ayios Nikolaos, and roughly following the north coast, one of the most beautiful of all the island's roads leads to the sleepy town of Sitia, technically Crete's fourth city after Iraklion, Khania and Rethimnon. Sitia is in fact less of a centre these days than Ayios Nikolaos and has few monuments or special points of interest, but it is agreeable in its atmosphere and could well be worth a stay. From here, one can go vaulting onwards to the furthest east, to Vai with its indigenous but over-rated palm-grove and to Kato Zakros, extremely remote but nevertheless the site of the fourth great Minoan palace. This whole eastern end of Crete is rich in Minoan sites and has contributed many items to the Archaeological Museum of Iraklion and the museum at Ayios Nikolaos.

The resort of **Ierapetra** on the southern coast is a place much visited by package-tourists. It may be reached from Ayios Nikolaos, by following the Gulf of Mirabello and then striking due south; or by travelling diagonally southwest from Sitia. There are interesting places to see on these routes, but Ierapetra itself is not particularly rewarding. It is a medium-sized town of little charm, but it does have a long beach and a good winter climate, and package holiday hotels are thick on the ground.

AYIOS NIKOLAOS

One of the great delights of Ayios Nikolaos is the first glimpse of the feature that has made the town its fortune, the small deep-water lake at its heart, enclosed by dramatic cliffs and linked to the sea by a narrow artificial channel. The little bridge across this channel, joining the two parts of the front, is the epicentre of Ayios Nikolaos. Around this hub, and the cheerful port on the seaward side, there has grown up a

newish town, which is very busy in the tourist season.

The journey from Malia to Ayios Nikolaos is short and quick. As it follows the last stretch of the north coast strip, the Old Road gives access to one or two seaside places like Sisi and Milatos, still fairly out-of-the-way but destined, it would seem, to achieve resort status. Then both Old and New Roads turn inland and climb over a mountain ridge before descending past Neapolis. This fair-sized town was the administrative centre of the prefecture of Lasithi until recent years, a role which has

now passed to Ayios Nikolaos. At
Driros, very near Neapolis, there
are remains of an important
Greek temple. There is also a
road due east, which descends
steeply and through many bends
to Elounda, offering magnificent
views of the Gulf of Mirabello
and the mountains rising
beyond. The main road runs
down southeast from Neapolis to
Ayios Nikolaos.
In Ayios Nikolaos itself, the front
consists mainly of hotels of
varying sizes. Around the
harbour, there are shops,
restaurants and discos, with
cafés densely packed on the

*Traditional ways continue: washing
wool near Ayios Nikolaos*

southeast side of the deep-water
lake, **Lake Voulismeni**. Two
roads with tourist shops and
boutiques—28 Octovriou
(October) Street and
Koundourou Roussou—lead up
to a little square, with greenery
and a war memorial. This is the
Plateia Venizelou.
The only other street of
particular interest is **Sfakianaki**,
which cuts across from the
harbour front to a small bay on
the eastern side of the town. The
bay is called **Kitroplateia**,

perhaps because citrus fruit was formerly handled here. Today, its rocky shore is used for swimming. There is a (paying) municipal beach on the south side of town past the bus station and a slightly better beach a mile (2km) further on. In terms of swimming, however, Ayios Nikolaos is a poor prospect and holidaymakers in search of beaches will do well to get right out of town during the heat of the day.

WHAT TO SEE

ARCHAEOLOGICAL MUSEUM
Konstandinou Palaiologou Street
This museum, past the lake on the seaward side, is Crete's most important archaeological museum after Iraklion, with a remarkable and growing collection. Exhibits, exclusively from the east end of the island, are pleasantly housed in a modern building more attractive from inside than out. Many digs have taken place in the east during the past 20 years and the pace of discovery remains rapid. As with Iraklion, some of the pleasure lies in linking particularly important or beautiful finds with their places of discovery, either visited already or on one's list of intended excursions.
Items on display include a collection of grave-goods from over 250 graves at Ayia Photia, beyond Sitia; and a collection of bronze daggers, one of them carefully bent over double like a folded tongue to render it harmless for the after-life.
Myrtos, west of Ierapetra in the

south, has contributed an extraordinary Early Minoan 'goddess', regarded as a masterpiece but looking, to a non-specialist, somewhat bizarre. The goddess is a bell-shaped pottery figure, with clay lumps for breasts, a triangle of pubic hair painted like a fish-net and a jug cradled in her arm. There are many examples of Vassiliki ware, that odd mottled pottery already noticed in the Iraklion museum. The most characteristic shape resembles a teapot with an elongated spout. The loveliest things of all, perhaps, come from Mokhlos, up on the northeast corner of the Gulf of Mirabello. The original finds here at the start of the present century included stone-jars of Early Minoan II and III periods, among the most glorious objects in the Iraklion museum. The museum has a wide range of Middle Minoan figurines from a number of peak sanctuaries and these, though highly simplified, demonstrate once again the Minoan gift for naturalism and the capture of the passing moment. It is fair to say, though, that the museum is a disappointment for the New Palace period—the best material from Zakros is, after all, in Iraklion. But the display concludes interestingly with a variety of exhibits ranging from an ivory crocodile to fine Daidalic sculpture.

Nightlife
Young people give top rating to **Studio Disco** on the front, where long-haired Nick the Greek is the DJ. Though now in his 70s he is the father of a young child.

Lipstick, a not dissimilar establishment, is two buildings along. For spectacular views at dawn, try the all-night **Cafeteria Bar Yachting Club**, out on the harbour mole.

Restaurants

There is a plethora of restaurants in Ayios Nikolaos and prices are generally higher than elsewhere in Crete. The **Cretan Restaurant** on the front (turn right at the bridge) is lavishly decorated with pot plants, textiles and stuffed birds and gets good reports even from locals. The **Trata** in Sfakianaki Street is a smartened-up taverna, and the **Itanos** on a side street going uphill from Venizelos Square is closer to the real thing. The **Faros**, well-situated on the Kitroplateia, is a pleasant place for a meal. The **Hotel Rea** has a Chinese restaurant and there are other eating places on the waterside just north of town. For an aperitif, the prettiest spot

is the new but traditional-style ouzo bar, or *ouzeri*, **O Vios Einai Oneiron** (literally, 'Life is a Dream') on a small side street off Sfakianaki. Design and woodwork are by the owner, the woman architect and carpenter Maro Dayiantis. There are delicious small eats to go with drinks, either in the courtyard or in a pastel-painted sitting room with lace curtains billowing at the windows when the north wind, the *meltemi* blows. Beer bars and fast-food joints abound in Odos 25 Martiou, (25 March Street) running off Sfakianaki one street behind Koundourou. George Koumakis's **Asteria Café** just by the bridge occupies a fortunate position; and local high school students, knowing a good thing, hang out at **To Kafeneion** (The Café), an eagle's nest above the lake on Nik Plastira Street.

Tourists and locals alike enjoy café life in Ayios Nikolaos

Shopping

Ayios Nikolaos has a range of
quite smart shops, selling mainly
jewellery and furs, intended to
cater for shopping as a holiday
pastime. The more expensive
shops are closest to the harbour.
Underneath Rififi, on the harbour
corner of Koundourou Roussou,
The Gold Shop (A Gerontis) has
both traditional Cretan designs
and modern gold jewellery. The
gold, as often on Crete, is bright
yellow. Koulendakis, almost
opposite, is very similar. Going
up the road away from the
harbour there are furs and
leather and plenty of knick-
knacks as well. There is the odd
supermarket for food and a
bookshop.

In a short side-street joining
Koundourou Roussou and
Oktovriou 28 Streets, the dress
designer Maria Patsaki has a
two-floor shop. The ground floor
displays Cretan ceramics and
jewellery. Upstairs, there is an
interesting collection of
traditional Cretan clothing, old
and new. This includes a range
of lovely white Cretan dresses,
for weddings, confirmation, etc.
There are rugs, fabrics for
bedspreads and much more.

WHAT TO SEE IN EASTERN CRETE

GOURNIA

The Minoan town of Gournia lies
a short way behind the sea,
climbing up out of a little valley
on to a knoll. At the top of the
knoll, there was once a complex
of larger buildings, not palatial
but probably occupied by
people of standing or authority.

There are remains of a public
courtyard here and a small
courtyard inside the 'official'
buildings. For the rest, the
township is made up of a warren
of tiny lanes, stepped and
cobbled and big enough only for
a laden donkey. The small
basements and semi-basements
undoubtedly had one more
storey on top—the evidence for
this lies in the stone steps which
the visitor will notice. Various
artisan dwellings have been
found here, so that our
impression is of a small
manufacturing town.
Gournia lies at the southern
extreme of the Gulf of Mirabello.

◆
ITANOS AND VAI

eastern Crete

Vai, on the far eastern coast, has
a fine beach and a grove of
palms of a kind peculiar to
Crete, producing inedible dates.
It also has masses of visitors,
lured by exaggerated tales of
the palm grove, and the beach
gets packed. Itanos, a little
further north, has fewer people
and the remains of a once-
important city-state. Dropping
south from Vai and Itanos, there
is an important Minoan site at
Palaikastron which will interest
mainly the specialist; and here
there are one or two places to
stay.

KRITSA

6 miles (10km) south of Ayios Nikolaos

Kritsa is a substantial hill village,
much frequented by day-visitors
and bus-tours. It is on the whole
attractive, despite the tide of
visitors, lured by the local

weaving. Good quality Cretan cloth and articles made up from it are manufactured here and sold, generally at a better price than in the towns. Leather goods are also plentiful.

◆◆
THE LASITHI PLATEAU

This is the largest of Crete's high, flat valleys and one of the most remarkable geological formations on the island. It is drained by a swallow-hole in winter and irrigated in summer by small, canvas-sailed windmills (assisted nowadays by many petrol-driven pumps). The famous cave which may have been regarded by the ancients as the birthplace of Zeus is just a few minutes' walk from the plateau.

Though too high for grapes or olives, Lasithi is a major agricultural area, specialising in potatoes, apples and cereal crops. Because it was ringed by a protective mountain rim, Lasithi was often a centre of revolt. In order to put a stop to this, the Venetians banned agriculture here for some 200 years—even though they badly needed the grain.

The main village in Lasithi is Tzermiado. The Diktean cave is reached from Psihro, either by walking or on a donkey. The cave was a major centre of pilgrimage for about 1,000 years from Middle Minoan times onwards and many votive objects have been found there. There are routes up to Lasithi from Metohi, Hersonisos and Malia on the north coast, from Neapolis and from Ayios Nikolaos. All have their own beauties and surprises.

In the mysterious Diktean cave, by tradition the birthplace of Olympian Zeus

LATO

2 miles (3km) from Kritsa

At the entry to Kritsa, a dirt road leads off right to Lato, a Dorian site perching on a high and rocky saddle. It boasts an acropolis at either end, and magnificent views down to the coast and back up to the Dikte Mountains. The ruins are massively solid, with a theatre and temple close to the normal point of entry. The saddle features a shrine, a rock-cut cistern and a set of steps rising beyond the courtyard in a manner reminiscent of Minoan theatral areas. The original entry to the city is down a walled and stepped alleyway to the left (it is in fact possible to reach this entry first of all by a lesser used and rather rough road, left instead of right at the final divide before the ruins). Above the flight of 'theatral steps' rising beyond the courtyard there is more evidence of massive building, some on fearsomely steep ground. In Lato, one has the sense of a people conducting an elaborate religious and cultural life behind the most rugged of fortifications. This is impressive enough—but it is the position which impresses most.

MONI TOPLOU

eastern Crete

This famous fortified monastery, now undergoing refurbishment, lies beyond Sitia and Ayia Photia. It has strongly defensive outer walls and a pleasing inner courtyard, with the abbot's quarters and cells on several levels. There is a well-known inscription here, part of the judgement pronounced in a border dispute between ancient Greek city-states in eastern Crete. There is also an important 18th-century icon in the church, regarded as a masterpiece. This illustrates the prayer beginning 'Lord, thou art great' and contains 61 tiny scenes, all full of exact detail.

THE PANAYIA KERA

Shortly before the village of Kritsa (see above) stands one of the most beautiful churches in

Crete, the Panayia Kera (Our Lady of Kera). Though neither large nor grand, this whitewashed building set among cypresses contains within its immemorial walls the most complete and best-preserved Byzantine frescoes on the island. It takes a surprisingly long time to work them out, but patience will be rewarded. It may also be helpful to buy a copy of Emmanuel Bourboudakis's pamphlet on sale at the church.

The frescoes of the Panayia Kera are one of the glories of Crete

The Panayia Kera has three naves. The paintings in the central nave are the oldest, done in two different stages during the 14th century. There are gospel scenes in the dome and on the vaulted roof of the nave—note particularly Herod's Feast and the Last Supper. Herod's soldiers are a tough-looking lot, contrasting with the elegance of the Venetian tableware in the picture. In the north aisle, the Second Coming is impressive, with its many haloed saints. There is a joint portrait of the church's founder and his wife. Both these aisles also have notably grotesque scenes concerned with the punishment of sinners.

The south aisle, the first you enter, is the brightest and offers a display of human emotions to which we can still respond. The pictures here tell the story of Mary's mother Anne and of Mary, showing her pregnancy and Joseph's sorrowful reaction. The experience of the church, if one can find the time and curiosity to make the most of it, is powerful and intimate at the same time.

◆◆
SITIA
43 miles (69km) east of Ayios Nikolaos
Sitia lies in an L-shape at the base of its own bay. The corner of the L is the central point, the Plateia Venizelou, with the main streets just behind it. From the *plateia*, as you face the sea, a long beach runs away to the right, backed by a scatter of tourist development and a valley with plastic greenhouses. To

Sitia, with its harbour backed by bright houses, is delightful

your left, running straight up northwards, is the harbour front, enclosed at the far end by a quay where the ferry docks. Steep and attractive streets, some with broad steps, climb up the hill behind among freshly painted houses. This part of town appears light and airy; upper storeys enjoy excellent views. The Venetians fortified Sitia but it never came to much (the Venetian fortress has now been restored). The town's greatest son was the epic poet Vincenzos Kornaros. The Turks destroyed Sitia and let it lie for two centuries. Then from 1870, it began to come to life again, achieving the extremely pleasant atmosphere that distinguishes it today. There has been an **Archaeological Museum** here since 1984 and there is a **Folklore Museum**, run by volunteers and not always

open when expected. The area is rich in grapes, generally on their way to becoming sultanas, and there is a lively sultana festival in mid-August.

SPINALONGA
north of Ayios Nikolaos
The remarkable island of Spinalonga may be reached on caique trips direct from Ayios Nikolaos, perhaps including a picnic and stops for swimming or by smaller, local boats from the attractive village of Elounda (see **Accommodation**, below). The main feature of Spinalonga is its massive Venetian fortress. Like the island-fortress at the mouth of Souda Bay, Spinalonga held out against the Turks long after Crete had fallen. It was eventually handed over in 1715. From 1903 to 1955 it was a leper colony, said to have been the last

in Europe. This gives an uneasy fascination to any tour.

♦♦♦
ZAKROS
eastern Crete

Zakros is a long way from anywhere and those who are only marginally interested in the Minoans may well be disappointed. But for some *aficionados*, this is the most inspirational of Minoan sites. The road to Kato (Lower) Zakros, the site of the palace, descends from Ano (Upper) Zakros, crossing slopes of a strange purplish hue. There is also a fine walk down through the ravine, though you will need precise instructions and should not venture here in bad or unsettled weather, as it is prone to flash floods. The ruins themselves lie close behind the sea, which has risen since Minoan days. Parts of the site are often semi-submerged.

The sense of distance and apartness conveyed by Zakros is largely an illusion. The palace was poised for trade with Egypt and the Middle East and Zakros must have been an important staging post. The very high quality of the artefacts found here (see gallery VIII in the Iraklion museum) indicates wealth and culture, at least in the palace community; the number and size of other Minoan sites in eastern Crete show that Zakros was by no means as isolated as it appears today. It had been thoroughly forgotten, however, even in Homeric legend, and was only rediscovered during the 1960s in the course of a celebrated dig by Professor Nicolas Platon.

Treasure after treasure was recovered from a palace which seems never to have been plundered and which is relatively easy for the visitor to understand today since the only ruins visible are those of the New Palace period.

A good beginning is to walk up to the higher part of the ruined Minoan town just behind the main palace; this provides an overview of the palace itself. It will quickly be apparent that it is laid out much like Knossos, Phaistos or Malia. There is a central courtyard, with sacred and cult chambers immediately to the west. Entry is by a gate in the northeast corner. Passing down a ramped passageway and turning right, the visitor will find a room which may have been used for ritual ablutions by those entering the palace. In front now, on the east side of the court, are what may have been the royal chambers, one of them constructed round a large cistern used for storage of water from an adjacent spring. Seawater and peasant plough have demolished the bulk of the ruins on this side.

Crossing the central court, the visitor will find on the west side the remains of a large hall and a light-well where the Zakros bull's head rhyton was found. Just near here, facing in a southwest direction, the visitor will see the ruined vestiges of a lustral basin and an archive room.

A treasury near the large hall remains contained the famous Zakros conical rhyton in rock crystal, smashed into hundreds of fragments and reassembled with infinite patience.

Accommodation

The road to Elounda strikes northwest along the Ayios Nikolaos front, with interesting views of inshore islands. Immediately on the edge of Ayios Nikolaos, on the right, there is a famous hotel, the **Minos Beach** (tel: 0841 22345). This was the first in Crete to use the central block and outlying bungalow concept and the hotel became the smartest place on the island. Today, though it has been displaced from this role, it still has the feel of a substantial and well-heeled country hotel with bits and pieces of post-modern art among its gardens— and with swimming that is typical of the area in being rather poor. Just a little further on, again to the right, comes the **Minos Palace Hotel** (tel: 0841 23801). A very swagger affair owned by the same company. Near by is a small Byzantine chapel with fragmentary decoration from the period of the Iconoclasts, when images of the human form were banned. The road soon climbs, offering fine views across the Gulf of Mirabello. Then it plunges down, reaching a turn to the **Elounda Beach Hotel** (tel: 0841

41412), successor to the Minos Beach as the smartest spot on Crete. This is built in block-and-bungalow style, very luxurious, but also making good use of ideas from Cretan vernacular architecture. There is one small beach and good swimming off the rocks into deeper water. Other hotels are now beginning to coalesce around this nucleus. A little further on is the **Astir Palace** (tel: 0841 41580), also an agreeable luxury class hotel. This is the most fashionable

Where the smart set once stayed: the famous Minos Beach hotel

corner of Crete, and the village of Elounda follows shortly. The harbour lies along one side of the large village square and boasts a miniature island with a house on it. There are plenty of rent rooms and the 'B' class **Kalypso Hotel** (tel: 0841 41367) on the front would make a pleasant place to stay.

Sitia offers the usual run of hotels—Nikos Andonidakis's **Itanos Hotel** (tel: 0843 22146) is very standard at the corner of the Sitia 'L'; a blockhouse known variously as **Sitia Beach** or the **Kappa Club** (tel: 0843 28821/4) lies a little way along the beach, monstrous in appearance but acceptable once you are inside. At the end of the beach are the **Bay View Hotel Apartments** (tel: 0843 24945), with genuinely good views back to Sitia. And if you enjoy extreme simplicity in a communal and floral atmosphere, then George and Katina Nikolorakis's **Seaside Pension** (tel: 0843 22815 or 22031), just behind the beach 200 yards (200m) past the bridge, may be the place for you – surely the friendliest spot in Crete.

Restaurants
In Sitia, the harbour front is the most animated part of town, with **Zorba's Taverna** considerably the largest restaurant. **To Steki**, by the bus station, however, seems totally genuine—pots of beans and hearty dishes seldom found in tourist venues. There are other restaurants in strategic spots along the roads out of town. For nightlife, **Zorba's**, fast moving towards monopoly, maintains another popular establishment.

PEACE AND QUIET

Crete's Wildlife and Countryside

Southernmost of the Aegean Islands, Crete is by far the largest, and has the most varied scenery, with idyllic coasts, freshwater marshes and the extensive and herb-rich *phrygana*, the latter being the open and grazed habitat so characteristic of most Greek islands.

Most unexpected of all, however, are the mountains, some of which rise to nearly 8,200ft (2,500 m) above sea level and remain snow covered long after the arrival of spring. The limestone which comprises many of the peaks has encouraged a rich variety of flowering plants, and gorges, carved through the ranges, harbour rare birds and mammals among the stunning scenery. Crete's position mid-way between Greece, Turkey and North Africa, makes it an ideal place to witness migration in spring and autumn, with many of the birds staying to breed. These supplement the numbers of year-round resident species, and compared to many other Greek islands, Crete's birdlife is surprisingly varied; almost every niche from mountain top to rocky coastal cliff has something to offer the birdwatcher.

Coasts and Seas

Dotted around the coastline, which comprises both sandy beaches and dramatic and inspiring cliffs, are quiet fishing villages and tranquil harbours. Visit any of these and the fishermen's catches and taverna menus will bear witness to the wealth of marine life that flourishes beneath the surface of the Mediterranean.

Do not expect to see much evidence of marine life on the seashore, however, because being effectively land-locked, the Mediterranean has a very small tidal range. Consequently, there are no rock-pools or mudflats to be exposed at low tide and birdlife on the seashore itself is rather limited. A variety of species of gulls is sometimes seen feeding along the strandline in search of carrion, but many individuals have learnt that the fish remains discarded at the ports and harbours provide a much better living.

The Mediterranean race of the herring gull is a frequent visitor to the coasts. Superficially resembling the herring gulls of northern Europe, these birds have striking yellow legs in contrast to the pink coloration seen elsewhere. Search among their numbers, especially in spring and autumn, and you may find an Audouin's gull, distinguishable by its smaller size and reddish legs and bill, or a slender-billed gull with its piercing pale eyes.

Coastal scrub often supports a variety of plants more typical of the *phrygana* habitat common throughout much of Crete. When in flower, they produce a dazzling array of colour, the months of March to May being best. Fortunately for the naturalist, this is also the best time of year for birdwatching, with migrant breeding species arriving from Africa to supplement the numbers of

Yellow-legged herring gulls are common around Crete's ports

resident species. Migrants on their way further north in Europe also frequently stop off around the coast to rest and recuperate. Coastal cliffs may harbour both Sardinian warblers and Ruppell's warblers, the latter looking extremely attractive with their beady red eyes and black heads with bold, white moustachial stripes. Cirl buntings and sometimes even Cretzschmar's buntings may lurk higher up the cliffs, while overhead, Eleonora's falcons, resident from May until September, dash through the air, catching migrant birds in flight.

Mountains, Cliffs and Gorges

Venture inland and the land soon rises up towards hills and mountains of dramatic proportions. This rugged side to the island's landscape is often overlooked by those tourists who linger on the beaches but it richly repays a visit: the scenery is dramatic and inspiring, with many of the summits rising to 6,500ft (2,000 m) or more above sea level, and the plants and animals to be seen in the remote regions are fascinating and varied.

The presence of mountains has been an important factor contributing to the diversity of the island's flora. While the plants of lowland Crete are often typical of other Greek islands, of those that grow on the mountains, a significant number occur nowhere else in the world. Many of the mountains' birds would also be out of place on most other Aegean islands, and the sight of eagles and vultures adds to the sense of isolation. Many of the peaks are composed of limestone, a rock which is vulnerable to erosion by the slight acidity of rainwater,

PEACE AND QUIET

and over the ages, rivers and torrents have carved spectacular gorges into many of Crete's mountains. Most famous of all is the Samaria Gorge, but others can be equally rewarding for the naturalist, their sides, like those of many of the steep mountains, being covered in shade- and moisture-loving plants. Higher up the mountain slopes, many of the plants acquire the same rounded and spiny 'hedgehog' appearance found in the *garigue* of the Balearic Islands. Here and there, however, beautiful patches of *Chiondoxa cretica* flower freely where the snow has recently melted, along with the crocus, *Crocus sieberi*. Birds such as the beautifully marked alpine accentor feed quietly among the vegetation, while overhead, choughs wheel noisily through the air, their splayed wing-tips resembling fingers. Inaccessible crags and fissures provide secure nesting sites for golden and Bonelli's eagles, large birds of prey which can be seen soaring high in the skies on outstretched wings. Both species are highly territorial and will not tolerate individuals of the same species or of any other raptor, such as peregrine, anywhere near the nest site, and aerial battles can sometimes be witnessed by lucky observers.

Spring-flowering Crocus sieberi, *a beautiful flower of the upper slopes*

The White Mountains

Dominating western Crete, the White Mountains, or Lefka Ori, hold what is arguably the most impressive scenery on the island. Their peaks are among the highest, several exceeding 7,850ft (2,400 m) above sea level, and the white limestone rocks, from which they earned their name, encourage an incredible diversity of flowering plants. Immense gorges, such as Samaria, dissect these mountains, their inaccessible ledges providing nesting sites for eagles and vultures. Crossing the Plain of Omalos to the start of the Samaria Gorge, the visitor comes upon staggering views of the mountains, often snow-clad until late summer. Out of reach of man and his grazing animals, some of the more remote and inaccessible slopes are covered with relict patches of forest comprising funeral cypress, *Cupressus sempervirens.* Among these trees, which are supposed to resemble a funereal flame, grow holm oaks and Kermes oaks that harbour woodland birds such as short-toed treecreeper, chaffinch and great tit.

Because of the altitude, many of the plants found here flower later in the year than those of the lowland coastal regions. From May until July a profusion of flowers appears, many of which are endemic to Crete, some being unknown outside the White Mountains. Several species of orchids grow alongside beautiful patches of the paeony, *Paeonia clusii,* cyclamens, pinks, mouse-ears and crocuses.

The birdlife of the White Mountains is also rich and varied. Lower slopes support parties of chukars, close relatives of the red-legged partridge, and blue rock thrushes, while subalpine and spectacled warblers lurk in the cover of low bushes. Overhead, birds of prey such as peregrine, Bonelli's eagle, golden eagle and griffon vulture soar on the thermals, sometimes being joined by lammergeiers. In the air these rare and majestic birds are recognised by their immense wingspan and wedge-shaped tail as they soar effortlessly in the breeze. Like other vultures, they feed primarily on carrion, but have the remarkable habit of dropping bones, too large to break or digest whole, from a great height on to rocks, causing them to   shatter.

The lower slopes of the White Mountains are still forested, giving a glimpse of Crete as it once was

PEACE AND QUIET

The Samaria Gorge

Few visitors to the Samaria Gorge can fail to be impressed by its awesome scale. Carved over the millennia by rushing winter torrents, the gorge descends from the Plain of Omalos towards the sea and is home to a wealth of plant and animal life.

Although it is possible to walk the entire length of the gorge from May onwards, this lengthy journey should ideally only be undertaken by experienced trekkers and only then when arrangements have been made to be met at the far end. The terrain is tough-going and flash-floods are not unknown and have caused fatalities even in recent years. However, a short excursion into the gorge is thoroughly worthwhile and will yield many of Samaria's botanical treasures while posing no safety risk.

Since the shade and humidity of the gorge's walls encourage a lengthy flowering period, there are interesting plants to be seen throughout the spring and summer. Many of the species are specially adapted to these damp conditions, thriving particularly well where water trickles over the rocks. Bellflowers, pinks and specialities such as *Symphyandra cretica* and Cretan ebony sometimes cascade down the rockfaces, safely out of reach of nibbling sheep and goats.

Within the gorge itself, pines harbour migrant birds such as orphean warbler and redstart as well as resident short-toed treecreepers, the only species of treecreeper to be seen on the

The steep sides of the Samaria Gorge (above) have a rich variety of flowers including the Cretan ebony (below)

Phrygana

Centuries of occupation by man have had a marked effect upon the vegetation of Crete. As with many other areas around the Mediterranean, much of the evergreen woodland which once cloaked the region has long since been felled, leaving only relict patches of natural forest in a few gorges and on inaccessible mountain slopes. Man's domestic animals have also taken a toll on the landscape so that the colourful and shrubby *maquis* habitat, so typical of the French Riviera, is not widespread either and the resulting landscape, known as *phrygana*, is open and stony with only the occasional isolated tree to break the monotony.

Crete's climate has also influenced the vegetation of the *phrygana*: shade-loving plants cannot survive the hot, dry summers on the baking soils and even those species adapted to the harsh conditions generally wither by June. The winter rains induce new growth, however, and by the spring, the plants have burst into leaf and flower. To protect themselves from dessication and to deter grazing animals, many of the *phrygana's* plants have developed natural defences. Some produce leaves which are wax-coated to reduce water loss, and spiny species of mullein grow with hairy-leaved sages. Among these, showy species such as fritillaries, birthworts and tassel hyacinths appear, mostly to die back soon after flowering. Some of the *phrygana* plants are endemic to Crete, and especially attractive is the Cretan ebony, *Ebenus*

island. The shade which the trees cast on the woodland floor provides ideal conditions for the endemic Cretan cyclamen, while in more open areas, a variety of spring-flowering orchids grow among cistus bushes and the beautiful paeony, *Paeonia clusii*.

As the gorge descends towards the sea, small parties of crag martins can be seen flying to and fro in front of the rockfaces. In the skies above, alpine swifts dash at high speed through the air, and while you follow a party of these aerobatic birds with binoculars, griffon vultures may glide into the field of view. If luck is really on your side, lammergeiers (bearded vultures), Europe's largest birds of prey, may join them.

cretica, large clumps of which produce beautiful heads of pink flowers in spring.

Ocellated skinks and Erhard's wall lizards hunt for insects on the dry *phrygana* soil and boldly-marked chukars are sometimes heard calling. Where the vegetation is dense enough, Sardinian, spectacled, subalpine or even Ruppell's warblers may be found. Hillsides often have blue rock thrushes, males of which sometimes sing from rocky outcrops, and both ortolan and Cretzschmar's buntings might be seen. The latter two species are superficially similar and females are difficult to distinguish, but a good look at the colours of males should separate them. Although both have brick-red plumages, ortolans have a dull green head with a yellow throat, while Cretzschmar's have a blue head with red throat.

Spring Flowers

Come to Crete in the height of summer and the landscape of the uncultivated lowlands will be almost universally brown and lifeless. The soil is parched and the unremitting heat and lack of water will have shrivelled all but the hardiest of shrubs and evergreen trees. However, visit the island again in spring and things will be altogether different: the leaves are green and flowers in a multitude of colours greet the eye.

To understand this almost miraculous transformation you need to appreciate the nature of the Mediterranean climate, which shows striking seasonal variation. Winters are generally

Phrygana *habitat is rich in birds and spring flowers*

mild and wet but from late spring until autumn, sunshine is virtually guaranteed and rain is almost unknown. Plants take advantage of this predictable cycle, growing and producing their leaves in the winter and lying dormant during the summer. Many species flower in the spring, at the end of the growing season and before the onset of the summer drought, and shortly afterwards they wither away

above ground, reappearing only after the first autumn rains. To escape the arid summers, plants have developed a number of strategies: underground tubers, bulbs and rhizomes are common and many species are annual, that is they live only one season, germinating in the autumn. However, what is true for lowland Crete is not necessarily true for the mountains, since altitude has a profoundly modifying effect on the climate. With over 1,500 species of plants to be found in Crete, there is no shortage of flowers to be seen in the spring and from March to June, tulips, poppies and flaxes adorn the fields. Some species, such as the crown anemone, *Anemone coronaria*, tassel hyacinth and many of the orchids, are widespread in the eastern Mediterranean, while others have a more restricted distribution.

Because of Crete's isolation as an island and its variety of habitats, around 100 species are endemic, that is they are found nowhere else in the world. There are

PEACE AND QUIET

endemic species of friar's cowl, birthwort, tulip and pink, but one of the most attractive is the cyclamen, *Cyclamen creticum*. Preferring to grow under the shade of trees, the leaves sometimes form little carpets and the delicate white flowers appear in March and April.

Plains and Agricultural Land

In contrast to the barren and stony hillsides with poor soils, many of the lowland valleys and plains are comparatively fertile and where an adequate water supply persists throughout the summer, a wide range of crops is grown. That most characteristic tree of the Mediterranean, the olive, is as widespread today as it has been for centuries and lemons, carobs, figs, almonds and even corn are also commonly grown. The cultivated fields provide feeding grounds for larks and pipits, while the leafy shade of orchards and olive groves is ideal for shrikes and warblers.

Warmth and sunshine are not in short supply but water, however, is a decidedly scarce commodity. Men go to great lengths to ensure a permanent irrigation supply, and nowhere more so than on the Lasithi Plain in eastern Crete. Surrounded by mountains, the area is famous for the water-pumping windmills which dot the mosaic of fields and keep them green and lush all year round.

By day, geckos and wall lizards scurry among the ground vegetation, while chameleons are occasionally seen sitting motionless and camouflaged in the branches of shrubs and trees. After dark, balkan whip

Cretan water-pumping windmills irrigate the Lasithi Plain

Green toads are strictly nocturnal

snakes and cat snakes venture out of cover in search of a meal, and boldly marked green toads patrol for insects.

Recently tilled fields are the haunt of skylarks, short-toed larks and exotic looking hoopoes that probe the soil with their long beaks. Although their black and white barred wings make them conspicuous in flight, they can be extremely inconspicuous on the ground as they shuffle along the furrows. Tawny pipits, wheatears and black-eared wheatears also prefer these open fields where insects are easy to find, and, in spring, males of the latter species are especially resplendent with their black, white and fawn plumage. Overhead wires and dead branches provide ideal perches for colourful bee-eaters who launch themselves into the air after insect prey. Their liquid calls are a familiar sound in lowland Crete in spring, and where sandy banks have been left undisturbed, they excavate long nesting burrows into the soil, colonies of half a dozen or more sometimes being found in one site.

Marshes and Saltpans

Around the coast of Crete, and especially between Iraklion and Sitia, several small areas of marshes and saltpans offer a habitat which contrasts markedly with the arid interior of the island. Wetlands, not only on Crete but throughout the eastern Mediterranean as a whole, are coming increasingly under threat from disturbance and tourist development. Hopefully, with a growing awareness of their importance both in terms of the island's ecology and as a lure to naturalist holidaymakers, the authorities may yet recognise their true value.

Marsh frogs and dice snakes are constant residents of the

A migrant wood sandpiper

marshes but the species of birds vary throughout the year. From early spring until the summer, a variety of migrant waders, including greenshank, wood and marsh sandpipers, little ringed plovers and little stint might be seen. The length of their legs determines how deep they can wade in the water, but by contrast, the depth of water presents few problems for black-winged stilts. They have such long legs that they can wade almost anywhere and if they get out of their depth, they resort to swimming.

Little egrets, elegant with their pure white plumage and long plumes, sometimes feed among the smaller waders. Purple herons, however, prefer to stay in the cover provided by reedbeds and other aquatic vegetation, and little bitterns, which are equally secretive, are seldom seen except in flight. Great reed warblers are bolder, however, and often sing their loud, guttural song from the tops of the reeds.

The evaporating, briny waters of saltpans are too hostile an environment for most aquatic creatures to survive. However, brine shrimps and brine flies both thrive under these conditions and their numbers provide a feast for both stilts and avocets, the latter being elegant, black and white birds with long up-turned bills with which they

A colourful milky orchid

scythe the water in search of
prey. As the water finally dries
up, the surface of the cracked
mud attracts short-toed larks,
Kentish plovers and pratincoles.
Despite their swallow-like
appearance both on the ground
and in flight, pratincoles belong
to the wader family, but unlike
other species in this group
they generally catch food on
the wing.

Orchids

Crete is justly famous for its
spring flowers, and in particular
for its native, wild orchids,
several of which are endemic to
the island. The list of orchids is
long, 20 or more species often
being recorded by visitors in a
week in April, with the variation
in their appearance almost

PEACE AND QUIET

endless. Some of the species occur in a variety of forms and it will come as no surprise to learn that many lovers of wild orchids pay regular spring homage to Crete to delight in nothing but its wealth of orchids.

Part of the fascinating lure of orchids comes from their appearance, the flowers often being a beautiful shape and colour. Some are fragrant and thereby attract pollinating insects, but many others do so by mimicking insect members of the opposite sex. In the bee orchid family, in particular, this is most highly developed, the furry lower lips of the flowers often looking extremely life-like.

The life history of orchids is also intriguing since in most cases, seeds will not germinate successfully if a partnership with a special fungal mycelium has not developed. Orchids are generally slow-growing, with sometimes as much as five years elapsing between germination and the appearance of leaves and flowers above ground.

On the open *phrygana* habitat, characterised by stony ground with scattered clumps of low vegetation, half a dozen or more species or forms of the genus *Ophrys* (bee orchids) can be found, including the endemic Cretan ophrys. Spikes of violet limodore prefer to grow where there is a little shade and are sometimes found in the company of dense-flowered orchids, whose thin, compact spikes of small white flowers can be difficult to spot.

The genus *Orchis* is also well represented on Crete by plants with often bizarre names like

Spitzel's orchid

monkey orchid, naked man orchid and bug orchid. Grassy patches often support the beautiful milky orchid, whose flowers resemble little dolls in brightly coloured dresses, while at higher altitudes, Spitzel's orchids produce flower spikes of a rich purple colour. The giant orchid, which more than lives up to its name, also grows on Crete, but since it flowers early in the year it has often withered to a brown spike before most visitors arrive.

Spring Migration

Lying less than 250 miles (400km) from the coast of North Africa, Crete is an ideal 'stepping-stone' for migrant birds heading north across the Mediterranean after a winter south of the equator. From March until May, thousands of birds pass through the island and, depending upon the prevailing weather conditions, many stop off to feed and replenish their reserves. Some of the migrants fly no further than Crete itself and, compared to most other Greek islands, its list of breeding species is rich, but many others continue the journey to northern Europe. Among the first to arrive are yellow wagtails, long-tailed birds which haunt fields and marshes on migration. At first, the observer may be confused into thinking that several species are present, but in fact yellow wagtails occur in a variety of colour forms or races, each one of which breeds in a different part of Europe. To distinguish them, you must study the head pattern carefully, but since these charming little birds are extremely active this is often easier said than done.

Even on migration, birds are attracted to the habitat to which they are normally accustomed and so, not surprisingly, marshes attract waders, terns and ducks. Garganey, drakes of which have elegantly marked head patterns, dabble among the vegetation, taking to the wing at the slightest danger, when the blue wing-panels and characteristic 'rattling' call help with their identification. Waders such as wood sandpipers, on the other hand, are often more confiding, allowing excellent views of their smart, spangled plumage. Around the coasts, olive groves and even small patches of vegetation may harbour warblers and chats in spring, the best time of day for searching being just after dawn. Since passerine birds generally migrate by night and make for cover at the first sign of light, coastal bushes are often the first opportunity they have to rest. If they are not disturbed, they will

Garganey haunt Crete's marshes in March and April

stay here for several hours before they gradually drift off northwards, and shrikes, subalpine, Bonelli's and willow warblers, and pied and collared flycatchers are all regularly seen. Later in the day, things become quiet as the migrants disperse, but there is always a chance of seeing a party of bee-eaters flying in off the sea.

Chameleons

Islands normally have comparatively fewer species of animals than adjacent areas of mainland, this being particularly true of terrestrial creatures, such as reptiles, which cannot fly. However, partly because of its size and partly due to the geological history of the Mediterranean, Crete has 12 resident species of snakes and lizards, including one, the chameleon, not found anywhere else in Greece.

Chameleons prefer bushes and trees even where conditions are rather arid. Their superbly camouflaged bodies can change colour to suit the exact hue of the surroundings, making them extremely difficult to spot. This camouflage not only serves to protect them from enemies, however, but also to render them inconspicuous to their insect prey.

When an insect is located with the aid of its fabulously ornate and swivelling eyes, the chameleon inches forward with extreme stealth and when in reach flicks out its long, sticky-ended tongue. By contrast with its slow-motion movement, the action of the tongue is like lightning and the prey is caught in the blink of an eye.

Found nowhere else in Greece, the chameleon is a common resident of scrub in lowland Crete

SHOPPING

Crete produces some handsome
and individual craft items and
any number of tourist souvenirs.
But in general shopping does not
figure outstandingly among
holiday activities. There is too
much else to do and too little in
Crete that is really exceptional.
Weaving is the most visible and
colourful of Cretan crafts. It is
practised particularly in the
mountain villages of Kritsa and
Anoyia. Colours are often very
striking; materials range from
relatively suave to awesomely
prickly. The best buys may be
bedspreads, rugs or sturdy
shopping bags. Greek shoulder
bags are also attractive. In Crete
there is a special variety used by
shepherds, with a draw-string to
pull the bag tight and woollen
cords to go over both shoulders
like a small knapsack. Highly
recommended. Old woven items
are also available in some
specialist shops—very beautiful
and very expensive.

Lace is still made in Crete but
many of the old stitches appear
to have been lost or have
become unprofitable. Antique
lace, when available, can be
beautiful, though pricey. Boots
are still hand-made in Crete and
can be very fine (see
Rethimnon). There are locally-
made, wooden-handled clasp-
knives, too, with violent-looking
serrated blades and other
equally earthy products from an
island still predominantly
agricultural.

Jewellery has long been made in
Crete and here standards are
looking up remarkably. Where
once the main offering consisted

Handmade craft items for sale

almost entirely of crude replicas
of Minoan jewellery, there are
now individual modern items,
often in gold, alongside quite
high quality replicas. This
coincides with the arrival of
fashion boutiques in places like
Iraklion and Hersonisos.

FOOD AND DRINK

Food

For true Greek food it is
necessary to look to the host of
informal tavernas, often by
beaches and in seaside villages,
with umbrellas or bamboo
awnings and outdoor tables
closely crowded together; to the
estiatoria, fairly modest
restaurants found mostly in
towns, where a wider variety of
dishes is likely to be served; to
the *psistaria*, where lamb and
other meats are roasted on the
spit, wafting delicious smells into
the neighbouring air; and, lastly,
to the few rather more formal
restaurants in smarter parts of
towns.

FOOD AND DRINK

In all these it is possible to eat interestingly—though people do tend to complain of the quantity of olive oil. Others resent the fact that everything is served lukewarm—which is how the Greeks and many other people in hot countries like it. But these barriers drop away as one gets into the spirit of the island. The only real problem is that in the smaller places, down towards the end of the supply line, variety may diminish dramatically in high season. Greek starters are now well-known outside Greece and have even reached Crete which used not to go in for them. Taramosalata, smoked cod's roe purée, is of variable quality; tzatsiki is yogurt and cucumber, generally with lots of garlic. Melitzanosalata, literally aubergine salad, is often the most tasty of the dips. Meat dishes are generally simple. Souvlaki, chunks of meat on a skewer, is sold in restaurants and also as a fast food. Lamb chops with a few chips, or French fries (*paidakia*) are a common stand-by. So is chicken (*kotopoulo*) and of course eggs (one egg, *avga*; two eggs, *avgata*). Omelette is *omeleta*. Restaurants and tavernas may serve various kind of stew, among them *stifado*— beef with tomato and onion. There are also a number of baked dishes. Best known is moussaka—mince, aubergine and bechamel. Spit-roast meat is sold by the kilo, which makes it look more expensive on menus than it turns out to be.

Fish is good but expensive and often, likewise, sold by the kilo. Pick your own where possible, either in the kitchen or from the fridge. Red mullet (*barbounia*) are much revered. Swordfish (*ksifias*) and octopus (*ktapodi*) are good, and squid (*kalamari*) is excellent but can be expensive.

In Cretan restaurants, choose from a selection of traditional dishes

Vegetables are often very good; tomatoes are the summer staple. *Horiatiki* or 'village' salads consist of tomatoes, oil, onions, olives and anything else going, with a cube of fresh goat's cheese called *feta* resting on top. This makes a refreshing accompaniment to any meal. There are also good stewed vegetables. *Fasoulada*, green beans stewed in tomatoes, can be excellent.

Greeks are not generally big dessert eaters, but delicious, honey-rich pastries are widely sold. Find your local patisserie (*zacharoplasteion*) and all too probably you will be tempted by *baklava* (pastry, honey and nuts) or the equally fattening and delicious *kataifi* (this looks like shredded wheat).

Greek coffee is the same as Turkish, the water boiled up with the grounds in tiny individual pots and served in tiny cups. The coffee is thick and usually sweet. *Metrio*—or medium—is the normal degree of sweetness. *Sketo* means 'no sugar', *glyko* very sweet. Tavernas seldom serve coffee, and some establishments serve only Nescafé.

In the days before tourism, the proper place for a Greek man to take coffee was the *kafeneion*, often a small and dusty little room with upright, wicker-bottomed chairs and old men reading newspapers. Women were not particularly welcome. Some traditional *kafeneia* still survive, even in tourist areas, but foreign women are now treated as honorary men. There are also cafeterias of a more obviously European type.

Local wines can be excellent

Drink

Crete is a wine-producing and wine-drinking island. There are no amazingly high quality wines but some of the labelled Cretan brands are increasingly good and 'loose' village wines, sold by the kilo in restaurants (*ena kilo* is one kilo, *miso* is half, about the same as a litre or half litre bottle) can be satisfactorily soothing. Bottled wines from elsewhere in Greece are also available. There is red (*mavro*, meaning, literally, black), white (*aspro*), rosé (*kokkino*, literally red) and resin-tasting *retsina*, originally made in Attica but now produced in Crete too. Light continental beer is locally produced and widely drunk, and foreign beers are now also brewed under licence. The best known Greek aperitif is *ouzo*, a colourless, aniseed-flavoured drink which turns white when water is added. Cretans drink home-made *tsikoudia*, also known as *raki*.

ACCOMMODATION

This is a grape-based, distilled liquor, equivalent to French marc or Italian grappa, very strong and for some tastes much prefererable to ouzo. All aperitifs are served with some small morsel of food called *meze*, or *mezedes* in the plural. This can extend to specially-ordered snacks, grilled octopus or sardines, shell-fish, etc—often delicious though potentially expensive.

ACCOMMODATION

The key to understanding accommodation in Crete, and to much else besides, is the realisation that two systems of tourism and two distinct tourist economies flourish side by side. One is the world of the pre-booked package holiday, and the other belongs to the independent traveller. Both groups are on the whole well served.

The great volume of package holidays are taken in hotels. There are six grades of hotel: luxury, and then from A to E. By the time 'C' is reached, hotels are extremely simple, though usually clean and perfectly decent. Most of the big package hotels are strung out along the north coast beaches, or located in the north coast resorts. They are sometimes out of scale against their settings but generally acceptable inside. Some are very good and have all kinds of facilities. But while they are fine for sun and sea, they may isolate the visitor a little from Cretan life. Almost all these hotels are closed in winter. There is one particular style of hotel in Crete which has become

Elounda, near Ayios Nikolaos, is Crete's most luxurious resort

quite characteristic of the island. In this type, there will normally be a central building for reception, dining room, other essential services and a limited number of bedrooms. Most of the

bedrooms, however, are in bungalows or simple two-storey buildings, likewise described as bungalows, and almost always set among gardens. The first Cretan hotel on this pattern was the Minos Beach in Ayios Nikolaos. It was followed by the Astir Palace and Elounda Beach Hotels, both near the village of Elounda, a little north of Ayios Nikolaos. The Elounda Beach is regarded as Crete's leading hotel, and very fine it is too. Many newer hotels, generally described in this guide as 'block-and-bungalow', have been built in imitation of Minos

ACCOMMODATION/WEATHER

Beach and Elounda. Others, though, are simple blocks of the kind often found in Spain. 'Villas', ranging from well-appointed houses to new and rather charmless little dwellings, are also pre-let to package holidaymakers. Tour companies arrange in advance to operate them for the whole of a season and the villa comes as part of a package including flight and possibly hire-car. Independent travellers must naturally take things as they find them. In terms of accommodation, they may not find very much in July and August. Crete's high-season popularity has at the moment somewhat outstripped provision. But in winter, spring and autumn this is a marvellous way to visit Crete. The rugged landscape means that mass tourism has by no means reached every corner; the sense of discovery endures, and out of season, even in remote places, there is almost always somewhere reasonable to stay the night.

Some independent travellers will be sufficiently well-funded to stay in the better hotels. For them the package holiday hotels are a poor bet, since they are not geared up to single-night stays and may prove over-expensive. But there are decent hotels in all the towns, ranging from 'A' class downwards. There is usually a cluster of acceptable 'B' and 'C' class hotels around bus stations. There is also a growing network of small hotels in interesting and unlikely places.

The other great stand-by, particularly popular with backpackers and the young, is 'rent rooms'. There are numerous rooms to rent in every town and many villages and these are generally adequate, sometimes very pleasant. The hospitality and friendliness of owners can be a pleasure. But do see the room before taking it, agree a price and expect to pay extra for showers. People with rooms to rent will often approach you or you can enquire in any café or taverna. There is also a limited number of pensions.

WEATHER AND WHEN TO GO

Crete, the most southerly of Greek islands, has a robust climate, fresh and delicious in spring, very hot in summer, warm and serene in autumn and generally mild in winter—though capable of deviating conditions. Like almost all the Mediterranean, it can be very windy in summer. The *meltemi* blows hard out of the north for days at a time and there is a rarer and unpleasant wind which

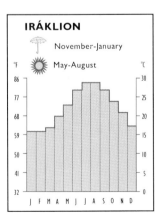

IRÁKLION

November-January

May-August

comes up from the Sahara laden with sand and dust. In winter, when it rains, it rains—then generally cheers up again. It can also be surprisingly cold in short bursts between November and February, a fact to which few concessions are made in cheaper accommodation. The mountains are snow-covered from autumn right through to late spring.

Summer clothing along the beaches should be very light. A jacket or jersey is only a marginal necessity and most people bring far more clothes than they actually use—even the smart set. In winter, it pays to pack on the opposite principle. Bring more warm clothes than you think you really should. Those planning to walk or sleep at higher altitudes should reckon with cold nights in summer and be properly equipped in winter.

SPECIAL EVENTS

There are many festivals and festivities, mainly local. The principal events are listed below. The year's major festival is the Greek Orthodox Easter, falling up to a month later than the Catholic/Protestant Easter. See also **Holidays** in the **Directory** section.

May
Khania Battle of Crete remembered in the last week in May in a series of events, including Cretan dancing in the Public Gardens.

July
Rethimnon Wine Festival in the town park for a week in late July.

August
Assumption of the Virgin, 15 August.
Iraklion Feast of St Titus, patron saint of Crete, 25 August.

NIGHTLIFE AND ENTERTAINMENT

Holiday Crete can boast a fair sprinkling of discos. Most hotels have their own and all the resorts offer a modicum of choice. Greek and specifically Cretan music can provide an experience out of the common run. The *bouzouki* is a kind of mandolin, originating on the mainland. Much of the best-

Visitors can enjoy folk music and dancing at a 'Cretan evening'

known Greek popular music is written for it, including the songs of Mikis Theodorakis. Bouzouki places are usually out of town, expensive, and start late, and among the few spots where you are likely to see Greeks drink at all heavily. The three-stringed lyre or *lyra* is the real Cretan instrument, powerful and plangent. Singers perform—and sometimes improvise—rhyming couplets called *mantinades*, a deeply traditional Cretan form. Crete has culture in abundance in its ancient and medieval art and architecture. The contemporary contribution is smaller. There are sometimes exhibitions of paintings in the church of Ayios Titus in Iraklion and various theatrical events, particularly in Iraklion.

There are two great popular entertainments. The first is the cinema. Films are usually shown in their language of origin, with subtitles. Many towns have outdoor cinemas in summer— operating after dark, of course. The other entertainment, in the bigger towns, is the *volta*, an evening stroll along one or two mutually agreed streets in which the whole populace appears to take part.

HOW TO BE A LOCAL

Cretans offer straightforward friendliness and it is churlish not to return it. This can happen even in crowded resorts, though women may have special problems here. There are now plenty of young men eager for involvement, to put it politely, with foreigners and this may involve active response. *Okhi* means 'No' and *figete* means 'go

In conservative Crete, the café is still largely a male domain

away'. *Neh*, surprisingly, means 'Yes'.

In the villages, when hospitality is offered, it is offered in the real hope you will accept it. This reflects a tradition unbroken

since the Homeric age and only gradually coming under threat. Sometimes you can be pressed to eat and drink—or to go on eating and drinking—when you really want to stop; and it can be difficult to beat a courteous retreat.

In villages, women will feel more comfortable if they dress modestly. In churches and monasteries, respectful dress is positively required, often by written signs—evidence that tourist behaviour has not always been up to the mark. The fact is that Crete is still a very conservative society. Topless swimming is now quite common, as is nude bathing, though technically illegal. It is, however, unwelcome to Cretans except where custom sanctions it. It is not good manners for people of either sex to strip off on a beach close to a country village.

CHILDREN

Children can have a wonderful time in Crete, provided they are given a day or two for adjustment and protected from the sun for a little longer at the start than may seem reasonable to them. The sea on its own is enough to ensure happiness at first; and for teenagers there are watersports—water-skiing or windsurfing—in many of the resorts. So far as interference or molestation is concerned, Greece is child-loving. Children are part of things in a way they are not in northern Europe— welcome in restaurants, bars and tavernas.

TIGHT BUDGET

Crete is a good place for those on a tight budget—as the presence of so many young people, many of them independent backpackers, amply demonstrates. They live very cheaply in that 'alternative economy' little frequented by package holidaymakers. For accommodation, there are 'rent rooms' and pensions (see above). Food can be very cheap, especially if you prepare it yourself or can get along on a simple diet of bread, fruit, cheese and tomatoes. Some of the young can make just a little money last a surprisingly long time. Older folk can cut expenses considerably by dipping into this economy from time to time. Tavernas are almost always more agreeable than hotel restaurants.

Vai beach: paradise for children

DIRECTORY

Arriving

By air The main international airport, serving the centre and east, is Iraklion, 3 miles (5km) from town, and scarcely able to cope with the summer crowds. It has a snack bar, a reasonable restaurant and a duty free shop for departures. There is easy connection with town by bus or taxi. Khania airport, 9 miles (15km) from town and the point of arrival for western Crete, is considerably quieter. There is a smaller airport at Sitia in the east, internal only, but good for island hopping.

By sea There are daily car and passenger ferry services from Piraeus, the port of Athens and the hub of island shipping. These go to Iraklion and Khania (Souda Bay). The arrival at Souda Bay, with views of the White Mountains above, is the most dramatic way of reaching Crete. There are regular arrivals in Iraklion via Santorini (Thera), a fine volcanic island north of Crete. There is a service from Githion in the Peloponnese to Kissamou Kastelli in the west and sailings—which may vary from year to year—eastwards to Rhodes and the Dodecanese Islands from Ayios Nikolaos and Sitia; and there have recently been some experimental connections between Crete and Italy.

Camping

In theory, camping is only permitted on official sites. Sleeping out on the beaches is still quite common, though, as one may readily observe in remoter spots like Souyia in southwest Crete. There are a number of organised camping sites in both larger and smaller places.

Car Breakdown

A warning triangle should be set out 55 yards (50m) behind the car, and flashing hazard lights turned on.

Car hire firms recommend that their customers contact them in the event of breakdown, and they will make arrangements. The police, the National Tourist Organisation and managements of large hotels are also helpful. Other motorists and just plain passers-by can be extraordinarily kind while mechanics are often more resourceful than in northern Europe.

ELPA, the Automobile Association of Greece, will help members of affiliated AIT clubs. Telephone numbers are: Iraklion, 081-289440; Khania, 0821-26059; Rethimnon, 0831-29950/28423; or call 104 (Automobile & Touring Club Emergency Road Assistance).

Car Hire

Car hire is now a major industry in Crete with the normal range of hire cars on offer, as well as four-wheel drive vehicles, often open-topped. International companies such as Hertz and Avis operate on the island; there are also numerous local companies. Many visitors arrange in advance to collect vehicles at the airport. Cars may be hired locally in resorts for a few days only or even a single day. Cars should always be looked over before they are

Mopeds can be hired in any resort

accepted since standards of maintenance and cleaning are far from uniform. Payment by credit card is preferred; if by cash, a large deposit will be required. A driving licence in force for more than a year will be requested; otherwise an international driving permit. All resorts have motor-bikes and mopeds for hire.

Chemist (see **Pharmacist**)

Crime

The crime rate in Crete is very low. There is some suggestion that foreign visitors are not above a little petty thieving, so normal prudence, at least, will be required.

Foreigners are strongly advised not to import or use drugs in Greece. Penalties for possession are considerable; and long sentences await those caught dealing. Casual camping and nude bathing are both technically illegal; see **Police**, below.

Customs Regulations

Visitors from Europe may bring in limited quantities of certain duty free goods, as shown below, slightly more generous allowances if tax and duty have been paid in EEC countries. Goods bought duty free: 200 cigarettes or 100 cigarillos or 50 cigars or 9 ounces (250g) tobacco; 1 litre spirits, 2 litres of drinks 22 per cent or less alcohol plus 2 litres wine; 50g perfume. Tax and duty paid: 300 cigarettes or 150 cigarillos or 75 cigars or 15 ounces (400g) tobacco; 1.5

litres spirits; 3 litres of drinks 22 per cent or less alcohol plus 5 litres wine; 75g perfume. For re-export, radios etc may be entered in owner's passport.

Domestic Travel

Air There are numerous flights each day between Athens and both Iraklion and Khania (for airports, see **Arriving**, above). Iraklion has flights to Rhodes, Mykonos, Santorini (Thera), Paros and Thessaloniki. Sitia offers more limited destinations.

Bus The service along the north coast's New Road, from Khania to Ayios Nikolaos, is fast and regular. Iraklion has four bus stations serving different quarters of the compass and a change of bus may necessitate a change of bus station, too. There

are good connections between the four 'nome' capitals and smaller towns in their areas. There is also an elaborate network of village buses, though these are likely to go into town in the morning and return in the afternoon, the wrong way round for many tourists. Tickets for longer journeys should be bought at the bus station, for shorter journeys on the bus.

Taxi These are reasonably priced and readily available. Two or three people travelling together may well find taxis handy for whole or half-day excursions—but do agree the price with the driver beforehand. Villages have special country taxis, marked *Agoraion*—in the Greek alphabet—and these make up for any gaps in the bus service.

Ferry There are numerous ferries from Piraeus and other

A donkey is the only transport to some places off the beaten track

islands (see **Arriving**, above).
Crete's own island
dependencies, notably Gavdhos
off the southwest coast, can also
be reached by sea.

Car
Documents (and extras) required
For car hire: Valid driving
licence and, probably, passport.

Age policy varies but for most
companies you must be 23 or
over.
For driving own car: To have
reached Greece, unless you
have stayed in EEC countries all
the way, you will probably have
needed an international driving
licence, *carnet de passage de
douane* and green insurance
card (without which your cover

On the road near Phaistos: the independent motorist can enjoy Crete's most spectacular scenery

will be third party only). Vehicle registration documents should also be carried. Check special requirements for countries en route.

For Greece, the vehicle should have a nationality plate or sticker; first aid kit; fire extinguisher; and a red warning triangle.

Entry formalities

The government is anxious that foreigners should not sell their vehicles during their stay. Your car will be entered in your passport on entry to Greece, causing problems if for any reason you have to leave without it.

Driving in Crete

This is certainly the easiest way to see the island but not as easy as all that. The New Road along the north coast is fast and modern. Roads to other towns and all major historical and archaeological sites are asphalt and the number of dirt roads is dwindling annually, if a little fitfully, as modernisation progresses. Most of the dirt roads are now fine—but there are hazards. Potholes may be impressive, especially if there are road works anywhere near. Winter rain and landslips can mean that edges of otherwise well-maintained roads disappear rather suddenly. Very minor roads still sometimes give up unexpectedly. And some of the gradients are steep, with little or no protection. Greek drivers expect you to blow your horn as you approach blind corners. They do not use their rear mirrors excessively and you are meant to hoot before overtaking. In summary, the experience is exhilarating but it is important to drive carefully and be ready for almost anything.

Insurance

Comprehensive cover is recommended both for own and

hire cars. Insurance giving cover for injury, hospitalisation, and 'Fly-Home Medicare' is also desirable for holidaymakers.

Petrol
Plentiful in towns but may be harder to find in rural areas. If you are planning a longish trip in remote parts, it is best to start with a full tank. Greece is one of the more expensive European countries for petrol. It is illegal to carry petrol in cans in vehicles.

Road signs
Road signs follow standard European conventions though there may be some additional signs in Greek only. Place names on signposts are usually given in the Latin as well as the Greek alphabet. Spelling normally follows the new phonetic version (*eg* Festos for the more customary Phaistos) and is not always immediately obvious.

Seat belts
Seat belts must be worn in front and rear seats and children must sit in the rear. There are on-the-spot fines for failure to comply.

Speed limits
40kph in towns (25mph); 100kph elsewhere (62mph).

Walking Crete offers some of the best walking in Europe, ranging from strolls through rich landscapes to arduous trails high among limestone crags. Walking in Crete is also a wonderful way to meet rural people. Some of the most used trails are waymarked with paint splodges, but people attempting the harder walks should be advised that experience really is required—as well as good

boots. Beginners will find that lesser-used paths dwindle and disappear and Cretan mountains are not a good place to get lost. Good footwear is vital for the popular Samaria Gorge walk.

Electricity
Crete runs on 220 volts AC. Supplies in rurual areas are unpredictable.

Embassies and Consulates
Embassies (all in Athens):
British: 1 Loutarchou Street, 106–75 Athens (tel: 723 62 11)
US: Leoforos Vas. Sofias 91, 115–21 Athens (tel: 721 29 51)

Canadian: Gennadious 4,
Ypsilantou, 115–21 Athens (tel:
723 95 11).
British Consulate (in Crete):
Dimokritias 338, Iraklion (tel: 22
40 12 and 23 41 27).

Emergency Telephone Numbers

The standard number for all
emergencies is 100.

Entertainment Information

Hotel desks are well informed
about local events, as is the
National Tourist Organisation
(NTO or EOT, see **Tourist
Offices**, below).

Entry Formalities (see also
Domestic Travel, subheading
Car)

Visitors from Britain require
passports or British Visitors'
Passport. Visitors from EEC
countries issuing identity cards
require only these. Entry is for
three months, generally
renewable. Eastern bloc visitors
are normally allowed entry for
two months only in the first
instance. Visitors from the United
States and Canada do not
require visas.

Guide Books

Among the many guide books on
Greece, a fair number are
devoted to Crete on its own.
Since the island is so
extraordinarily rich in art and
architecture, flora and fauna and
all manner of other matters, the
fuller the guide the better for
those who intend a longer stay or
detailed touring. The *Blue Guide
Crete*, in the new version by Pat
Cameron, A. & C. Black, London,
W.W. Norton, New York, is
probably the fullest. John
Fisher's *Rough Guide to Crete*,
Harrap Columbus, also packs in
a surprising amount. It is
addressed mainly to younger
readers but its insights into
Crete and its strong desire to
understand Cretans will be
generally appreciated. Some
find GROC's *Candid Guide to
Crete*, Ashford Press Publishing,
useful and very funny. The key
guides for walkers are:
*Landscapes of Eastern Crete/
Landscapes of Western Crete*,
both by Jonnie Godfrey and

*Information on local events is
available in many hotels*

Elizabeth Karslake,
Sunflower Books.
On Crete in general there is an
enormous literature. A
bibliography covering several
aspects will be found in *Crete,
its past, present and people*,
Adam Hopkins, Faber and Faber
(revised imprint 1989).

Health Regulations

For visitors from Europe and
North America, there are no
special health regulations
affecting Greece. Smallpox
vaccinations may be required
for visitors from some other parts
of the world.

Holidays, Public and Religious

New Year's Day: 1 January
Epiphany (exchange of
Christmas presents): 6 January
Kathara Deftera ('Clean
Monday'): celebration at entry to
Lent, preceded by three weeks
of lively carnival
Independence Day: 25 March
Labour Day: 1 May
Greek Orthodox Easter: Friday
to Monday, falling up to a month
later than Catholic/Protestant
Easter
Ascension Day: date determined
by Easter
Assumption of the Virgin: 15
August
Okhi or 'No' Day: 28 October
(celebrates Greece's one word
reply to Italian ultimatum, World
War II)

Lost Property

Report lost passport to police
and contact consulate. Loss of
travellers' cheques should be
reported to the police; contact
the consulate only if stranded
without money.

Money Matters

The unit of currency is the
drachma—plural drachmes—
abbreviated to Drs. There are
coins of 1, 2, 5, 10, 20 and 50 Drs,
and notes of 50, 100, 500, 1,000
and 5,000.
On entry, unlimited foreign
currency and travellers' cheques
may be imported, though
anything over £300/US$500
should be declared, enabling
you to take it out again. You are
not allowed to take in, or out,
more than 3,000 Drs in Greek
currency. This is a small sum and
means you will have to obtain
more almost immediately.
Banks, and the Post Office, which
now offers an exchange service
for both cheques and foreign
currency, have the most
promising rates. For banking
and post office hours, see
Opening Times, below.

Opening Times

Greece is a law unto itself over
opening times, perhaps because
they are so complicated. The
best one can do is state official
hours and conventional norms—
alongside the warning that
almost everything needs
checking on the day.
**Archaeological sites and
museums** Hours differ from site
to site, from year to year and
according to the season.
Summer hours, mid-March to
mid-October, are longer than
winter hours. Sunday hours are
shorter than on a weekday. Sites
and museums close entirely on
some bank holidays and open for
Sunday hours on others.
Normally, the Iraklion
Archaeological Museum is
closed on Mondays; Knossos,

It is advisable to check opening times for sites such as Knossos

Phaistos, Malia and Zakros are open daily though for differing periods; Ayia Triada is closed on Fridays. Some sites remain open over the lunch hour.

Monasteries These almost always close their doors during the afternoon, usually from 14.00 to 17.00.

Banks 08.00 to 14.00 Monday–Friday, with perhaps one duty bank re-opening its change desk from 17.30 in major resorts.

Post offices Main post offices (in nome capitals): 08.00 to 20.00 Monday–Friday; special post office caravans in tourist areas also open 08.00 to 20.00 Monday–Saturday, plus 09.00 to 18.00 Sunday. Lesser post offices generally Monday–Friday, 07.30 to 15.30. Post office exchange facilities are available at slightly different hours: normally 08.00 to 13.30 in post offices, in caravans 08.00 to 20.00. Monday–Saturday, nothing on Sunday.

Shops Business begins early with shops opening up progressively from about 07.00. Officially, opening hours for most types of shop are 08.00 to 14.00, Monday and Wednesday, 08.00 to 15.00 Saturday. But on Tuesday, Thursday, Friday, 08.00 to 13.00 only (food shops 13.30) with afternoon opening, 17.00 to 20.00 in summer, 16.00 to 19.30 in winter. In major resorts, however, increasing numbers of shops stay open over the lunch hour.

Personal Safety

Sunburn is the worst hazard and the most common complaint. Care must also be taken with swimming when the *meltemi* is blowing; and there are one or two underwater hazards worth mentioning—sea urchins in particular. Some kind of footwear may be a good idea in any event when swimming off sandy beaches. There is a poison fish which buries itself under the sand, with only its venomous spines protruding. If you should tread on one, medical help is required immediately.

Pharmacist

Found only in the larger towns, pharmacists play a greater part in medical matters than they do in Britain. They are able to dispense directly some drugs and medicines only available on prescription in other countries. Codeine is banned in Greece; so are liquid painkillers. One pharmacist at least always stays open round the clock in the larger towns—details of roster posted in windows.

Places of Worship

The official religion is Greek Orthodox, with churches and chapels in great abundance. Services are often extremely beautiful and feast day services in particular are among the most important popular events on a devout island. There are Catholic churches in Iraklion, Khania, Rethimnon and Ayios Nikolaos. There are no other Christian variants on Crete, nor

Greek Orthodox services are held throughout Crete in churches like this one at Ayia Varvara

is there a synagogue or active mosque.

Police

Police attitudes seem to shift with changing regimes and are currently friendly and helpful— though inevitably perhaps the police are fonder of the outwardly respectable than they are of backpackers; there is some sensitivity if an area appears to be 'going hippy'.

major post office (recognisable by its yellow sign); major holiday towns and resorts may also have post office caravans, open for longer hours and there is a network of lesser post offices in smaller places. Stamps are sold in post offices, of course, and also in kiosks—*periptera*—often with a small mark-up. The Poste Restante system is widely used in Greece. Send letters to the addressee, Poste Restante, at any town and they can be collected, on proof of identity, for a small fee. Post boxes are yellow. *Esoteriko* means inland, *exoteriko* means abroad.

Senior Citizens

Crete respects and enjoys its own older people but is not well adapted to the specialist needs of elderly visitors—nor, indeed, to the needs of the disabled. Hotels are short on ramps, for instance, and outside the hotel most places seem to be steep or rocky or alarmingly full of traffic.

Student and Youth Travel

Crete is a good place for young people, as many have discovered. There are campsites, a good range of cheap rooms and youth hostels in Iraklion, Khania, Malia, Ayios Nikolaos, Ierapetra, Rethimnon, Sitia, Mirtios and Plakias. Obtain Youth Hostel Association documents in your own country before setting out. Simple food can still be cheap on Crete and there are (limited) opportunities for work.

Telephones

The international code is 00. For UK: 0044 followed by British code and number less initial

Nobody, however, should mess around with Greek policemen, particularly if indulging in sometimes tolerated but technically illegal activities like nude bathing or sleeping out. The Tourist Police, a separate branch of the police force, are invariably very helpful. They can be distinguished by their dark grey uniforms with patches in the form of national flags to indicate the languages spoken.

Post Office

Each provincial capital has a

zero. For USA: 001. Codes in Crete: Iraklion, 081; Khania, 0821; Rethimnon, 0831; Ayios Nikolaos, 0841; Sitia, 0843. Look for OTE (a separate organisation from the Post Office), where telephones are provided in cubicles. These are metered; you pay afterwards. Kiosks— *periptera*—often have metered telephones. In villages, the metered telephone will generally be in a *kafeneion*.

Time (local)
Greece is normally two hours ahead of Britain; one hour ahead of France and other western European countries; seven hours ahead of Eastern Seaboard Time, USA.

Tipping
Though the percentage given is sometimes quite small, Greece is a tipping country. Even the cinema usherette expects a contribution. Five to 10 per cent is appropriate in smaller restaurants (deposited on the table for table layers and lesser waiters, on the dish with the bill for the head waiter). Don't feel obliged to tip in village establishments where the owner is serving personally. Hotel dining rooms and the smarter restaurants generally include an extra 10 or 15 per cent service charge, on top of which you will probably leave any change. In hotels, tip porters and chambermaids. In bars and cafés, leave 5 per cent or so or apply the loose change principle. Taxi drivers, mostly owner-occupiers, do not expect tips, nor do they reject them.

After enjoying a meal out, it is customary to leave a tip

Toilets
Plumbing is fine in the modern hotels, casual to a fault elsewhere. A visit to one of the rare public toilets can be a fearsome experience; cafés are often a better proposition. Steel yourself, even so, for seatless ceramic rims, perhaps in

combination with dirty lavatory bowls and floors awash. In simple establishments, the waste paper basket by the toilet is there to collect used toilet paper.

Tourist Offices

Before you travel:
The National Tourist Organisation of Greece (NTOG), often known as the Greek National Tourist Organisation (officially in the USA), has much useful information. Offices include:
London: 4 Conduit Street, W1 ODJ (tel: 01-734 5997) New York: 645 Fifth Avenue, Olympic Tower, New York NY 10022 Montreal: 123 de la Montagne Sydney: 51–57 Pitt Street
On Crete:

DIRECTORY

Branches of the National Tourist Organisation—here also known as EOT (Ellinikos Organismos Tourismou)—are extremely helpful. Main offices: Iraklion, Xanthodidou Street 1, opposite Archaeological Museum (tel: 081-222 487); Khania, Akti Tombazi 6 (tel: 0821-26 426); Rethimnon, El. Venizelou Avenue (on beach) (tel: 0831 29 148); Ayios Nikolaos, Akti I. Koundourou 20 (tel: 0841-22537); Sitia, Iroon Polytechniou Square (tel: 0843-24 955).

No amount of tourism can spoil the essential beauty of Crete

LANGUAGE

Unless you know the Greek script, a vocabulary is not of very much use to the visitor. But it is helpful to know the alphabet, so that you can find your way around; and the following few basic words and phrases will help too.

Alphabet

Alpha	Aα	short a, as in hat
Beta	Bβ	v sound
Gamma	Γγ	guttural g sound
Delta	Δδ	hard th, as in father
Epsilon	Eε	short e
Zita	Zζ	z sound
Eta	Hη	long e, as in feet
Theta	Θθ	soft th, as in think
Iota	Iι	short i, as in hit
Kappa	Kκ	k sound
Lambda	Λλ	l sound
Mu	Mμ	m sound
Nu	Nν	n sound
Xi	Ξξ	x or ks sound
Omicron	Oo	short o, as in pot
Pi	Ππ	p sound
Rho	Pρ	r sound
Sigma	Σσ	s sound
Taf	Tτ	t sound
Ipsilon	Yυ	another ee sound, or y as in funny
Phi	Φφ	f sound
Chi	Xχ	guttural ch, as in loch
Psi	Ψψ	ps, as in chops
Omega	Ωω	long o, as in bone

Numbers

1	*éna*	10	*déka*
2	*dío*	11	*éndeka*
3	*tria*	12	*dódeka*
4	*téssera*	13	*dekatría*
5	*pénde*	14	*dekatéssera*
6	*éxi*	15	*dekapénde*
7	*eptá*	16	*dekaéxi*
8	*októ*	17	*dekaeptá*
9	*ennía*	18	*dekaoktó*
19	*dekaennía*	50	*peninda*
20	*íkosi*	100	*ekató*
30	*triánda*	101	*ekaton éna*
40	*saránda*	1000	*chília*

Basic vocabulary

good morning *kaliméra*
good evening *kalispéra*
goodnight *kaliníkta*
goodbye *chérete*
hello *yásou*
thank you *efcharistó*
please/you're welcome *parakaló*
yes *neh*
no *óchi*
where is…? *poo íne?*
how much is…? *póso káni?*
I would like *tha íthela*
do you speak English? *milate anglika*
I don't speak Greek *then miló helliniká*

Places

street *odós*
avenue *leofóros*
square *platía*
restaurant *estiatório*
hotel *xenodochío*
room *domátio*
post office *tachithromío*
letter *grámma*
stamps *grammatóssima*
police *astinomía*
customs *teleoniakos*
passport *diavatírion*
pharmacy *farmakío*
doctor *iatrós*
dentist *odontiatrós*
entrance *ísothos*
exit *éxothos*
bank *trápeza*
church *eklisía*
hospital *nosokomío*
café *kafeneion*

Travelling

car *aftokínito*
bus *leoforío*
train *tréno*

LANGUAGE

boat *karávi*
garage *garáz*
train station *stathmós*
bus station *stási ton leoforío*
airport *aerodrómio*
taxi *taxi*
ticket *isitírio*

Food
food *fagitó*
bread *psomí*
water *neró*
wine *krasí*
beer *bíra*
coffee *kafé*

Fish
lobster *astakós*
squid *kalamarákia*
octopus *oktapóthi*
red mullet *barboúnia*
whitebait *maríthes*
sea bream *sinagrítha*

Meat/poultry
lamb *arnáki*

chicken *kotópoulo*
meat balls *kefthédes*
meat on a skewer *souvlákia*
liver *sikóti*

Vegetables
spinach *spanáki*
courgette *kolokithía*
beans *fasólia*

Salads and Starters
olives *eliés*
yoghurt and cucumber dip *tzatsíki*
tomato and cucumber salad *angoúr domáta*
stuffed vine leaves *dolmádes*
'Greek' salad with cheese *horiatikí*

Desserts
honeycake *baklavá*
honey puffs *loukoumádes*
semolina cake *halvá*
ice cream *pagotó*
yoghurt *yiaoúrti*
shredded wheat and honey *kataïfi*
custard tart *bougátsa*

With a smattering of Greek, shopping for food can be fun

126

INDEX

ACKNOWLEDGEMENTS

The Automobile Association would like to thank the following photographers and libraries for their assistance in the compilation of this book.

J. CADY 80 Sitia.

J. ALLAN CASH PHOTOLIBRARY 21 Iraklion, 70 Souda Bay.

INTERNATIONAL PHOTOBANK 23 Market, 36 Knossos, 38/9 Matala, 41 Phaistos, 42 View from Phaistos, 49 Arkadı Monastery, 58 Carriages, 60 Handicrafts, 67 Samaria Gorge, 71 Ayios Nikolaos, 105 Cretan evening, 106/7 Taverna, 108 Vai beach, 111 Donkey, 112/3 Motoring, 114/5 Dancing, 120/1 Matala.

MARY EVANS PICTURE LIBRARY 15 Jason and the Argonauts, 18 Fighting Turks.

NATURE PHOTOGRAPHERS LTD 13 Knossos palace (R O Bush), 85 Herring gull (S C Bisserot), 86 Crocus, 87 White mountains, 88 Cretan ebony, 90/1 *Phrygana* habitat (K J Carlson), 93 Green toad (P R Sterrey), 94 Wood sandpiper (R Tidman), 95 Milky orchid (D T Ettlinger), 96 Spitzel's orchid (R B Burbidge), 97 Garganey (R Tidman), 98 Chameleon (M Bolton).

SPECTRUM COLOUR LIBRARY Cover Ayia Galini, 7 Spinning, 11 Fresco, 17 Wall painting, 25 Pottery, 26 Clay figures, 29 Venetian fortress, 30 café, 31 Ayia Triada, 33 Gortyn, 45 Rethimnon, 46 Shopping, 56 Khania, 62 Monastery, 64/5 Ayia Roumeli, 68 Loutro, 72/3 Washing wool, 75 Café, 77 Diktean cave, 78/9 Panayia Kera fresco, 82/3 Minos Beach hotel, 88/9 Samaria Gorge, 92 Windmills, 99 Souvenirs, 100 Food, 101 Gathering grapes, 110 Mopeds, 117 Knossos, 118/9 Church, 122 Sunset, 124 Iraklion.

ZEFA PICTURE LIBRARY (UK) LTD 50/1 Ayia Galini, 53 Aptera ruins, 54/5 Harbour, 102/3 Elounda.